Graph Data Science with Python and Neo4j

Hands-on Projects on Python and Neo4j
Integration for Data Visualization and
Analysis Using Graph Data Science
for Building Enterprise Strategies

Timothy Eastridge

www.orangeava.com

First published: March 2024
Published by: Orange Education Pvt Ltd, AVA™
Address: 9, Daryaganj, Delhi, 110002 **(INDIA)**

275 New North Road Islington Suite 1314 London,
N1 7AA United Kingdom **(UK)**

ISBN: 978-81-97081-96-5

www.orangeava.com

Dedicated To

My sons

May you always see beyond the data
towards a more whole and complete world

About the Author

Timothy Eastridge is an Insights Strategist known for innovation and thought leadership in integrating knowledge graphs with Generative AI and Large Language Models (LLMs). His expertise in extracting actionable insights from complex datasets positions him as a leader in transforming data into insights. Tim's innovative solutions have resulted in billions of dollars of suspicious activity reports (SARs) for a major bank related to the Paycheck Protection Program (PPP). He has also consulted with the United States Government's Pandemic Response Accountability Committee (PRAC), leading the team in the identification, prioritization, and indictment of fraudsters using a combination of unsupervised machine learning and recommendation systems.

Tim has also led GenAI projects in the private equity sector to deliver millions in value to clients by implementing graph neural networks (GNNs) to uncover alpha and new investment strategies. His mission is to help clients illuminate the hidden connections within data to reveal actionable insights.

About the Technical Reviewer

Siddhant Agarwal is currently leading Developer Communities for APAC at Neo4j. Formerly, he pioneered India's first fintech community as the 'Developer Relations Lead' at Open Financial Technologies, 100th unicorn of India. Prior to that, he spearheaded community efforts as a Program Manager with Google's Developer Relations team in India, overseeing programs like Developer Student Clubs, TensorFlow User Groups, Google Developer Groups, and Google Developer Experts. In 2019, he collaborated with the Ministry of Electronics and Information Technology, Government of India, to launch 'Build for Digital India,' engaging over 7,000 students in solving India's challenges.

He is passionate about design thinking and enjoys mentoring startups to enhance their UX and designs. Recognized as one of ACM's Distinguished Speakers, his career of roughly a decade has been dedicated to building, scaling, and growing developer and startup communities in India, launching ed-tech initiatives, fostering design innovation, and contributing to the startup ecosystem.

In 2021, he was nominated as a finalist for the CMX Community Industry Awards for his role in community building. As an avid public speaker, he has shared insights at over 1,000 national and international forums, reaching 300,000+ individuals.

Acknowledgements

This journey of writing *Graph Data Science with Python and Neo4j* has been an enriching experience, one that I could not have embarked on without the support and encouragement of many.

First and foremost, I extend my heartfelt gratitude to my data science peers. Your expertise and feedback have been invaluable. Your excitement, passion, and curiosity are an inspiration, and this book is a testament to the collective knowledge and spirit of our community.

To my family, thank you. A special thanks to my wonderful wife, who tolerated and supported my early morning writing sessions. Your patience, love, and belief in my work provided much-needed strength for this endeavor.

Lastly, I wish to acknowledge the global data science and open-source community. This book draws upon the wealth of open-source tools, shared knowledge, and collective wisdom of this vibrant community. Together, we are pushing the boundaries of what's possible, making a tangible impact on the world around us.

Thank you all for being part of this journey. Let's continue to explore, discover, and innovate for the advancement of data science and the betterment of humanity.

Preface

Who is this Book For?

The focus of Data Science is to extract actionable insights and intelligence from data. Graph Data Science is an important domain of Data Science that stitches together data architecture and design, data analytics, statistical analysis, and machine learning.

In *Graph Data Science with Python and Neo4j*, you will find a comprehensive analysis of data analytics with graph theory, accompanied by practical exercises that cover multiple aspects and domains of graph data science. Readers will grasp both the fundamentals as well as the practical experience to implement this form of data analytics on their own. The book covers topics in graph data science related to exploratory data analysis, supervised machine learning, unsupervised machine learning, recommendation systems, and more.

Whether you are new to data science or a seasoned veteran, you will find this book to be a refreshingly simple introduction and application of this form of analytics.

At its core, graph data science is simply an intuitive representation of connected data. This book will illustrate how we can leverage this intuitive, connected data design to supercharge our data analytics.

What this Book Covers

This book expands beyond a surface-level explanation and delves into the nitty-gritty details of network structures, graph algorithms, and similarity networks. This book provides a comprehensive understanding of graph data science concepts.

Chapter 1. Introduction to Graph Data Science

This chapter is an introduction to graph data science. It starts with the basics of graph theory and emphasizes the value of graph visualizations in making data insights accessible. It explores the synergy between data science, machine learning, and graph technology. Additionally, it introduces Python programming as a crucial skill for leveraging Neo4j's capabilities and sets a foundation for advanced graph-based analysis in the chapters that follow.

Chapter 2. Getting Started with Python and Neo4j

This chapter guides you through the initial steps of setting up your environment for graph data science with Python and Neo4j. It begins with a walkthrough of installing Python, followed by an introduction to the Cypher Query Language, which is used to interact with Neo4j databases. The chapter also introduces Neo4j's interfaces, providing clarity on how to navigate and utilize them effectively including how to establish a connection between Python and the Neo4j database.

Chapter 3. Importing Data into the Neo4j Graph Database

This chapter compares graph databases to traditional relational databases and speaks to the benefits of the Neo4j graph database. It introduces graph database terminology, providing a foundation for understanding graph data structures. The chapter also covers the basics of the Neo4j Cypher query language which is used to query and manipulate data in Neo4j. Finally, it guides readers through the process of importing data into Neo4j.

Chapter 4. Cypher Query Language

This chapter centers around crafting Cypher queries. It starts with basic MATCH, WHERE, and RETURN operations and moves to advanced techniques using COLLECT, CONTAINS, and EXISTS. It introduces the concept of counting relationships or "degrees" of nodes. This chapter contains a section on generating Graph Data Science (GDS) projections and creating "similar" relationships between nodes based on common attributes. Finally, the chapter covers Cypher query "explain" plans for optimizing query performance.

Chapter 5. Visualizing Graph Networks

This chapter dives into using Neo4j Bloom for graph visualization. The chapter begins with setup instructions. It explains rules-based styling as well as exporting data to CSVs for sharing and further analysis. The chapter also speaks to the integration of graph data with Power BI for advanced visual analytics, streamlining the process from setup to creating compelling graph visualizations.

Chapter 6. Enriching Data with ChatGPT

This chapter begins by introducing the ChatGPT technology which lays the groundwork for integrating AI-driven insights into graph data analysis. The chapter explores a patent dataset, showcasing how to uncover patterns and insights from a rich network of patents. The chapter explores enriching data using the ChatGPT

API in Python. Next, it details creating embeddings of patent summaries, a step crucial for understanding and leveraging the semantic content of patents. Finally, it concludes with techniques for reducing the size of vector embeddings, enabling their visualization with Plotly in Python.

Chapter 7. Neo4j Vector Index and Retrieval-Augmented Generation (RAG)

This chapter covers vector indexing in Neo4j, starting with the preparation of stock market text data for vector embeddings. It outlines the process of creating and storing these embeddings in Neo4j, demonstrating how to enhance the depth and utility of a knowledge graph with contextual data.

Chapter 8. Graph Algorithms in Neo4j

This chapter explores advanced graph analysis techniques, starting with centrality measures to identify the most influential nodes within a network. It then explores community detection algorithms, which segment graphs into closely connected clusters. The chapter also introduces network embeddings and graph neural networks which are cutting-edge methods that translate graph structures into numerical representations, facilitating machine learning applications on graph data.

Chapter 9. Recommendation Engines Using Embeddings

This chapter walks readers through the process of loading a patent database dump into the Neo4j Desktop environment. It introduces two approaches to building recommendation engines: 1) the Retrieval-Augmented Generation (RAG) approach and 2) the RetrievalQA approach. The RAG section explores how to enhance recommendation systems by integrating retrieval capabilities with generative models, while the RetrievalQA part covers question-answering models for more precise recommendations.

Chapter 10. Fraud Detection

This chapter discusses fraud detection analysis which is a common use case for graph databases due to the nature of interconnected data. It discusses the importance of data engineering and the processes involved in enriching the fraud dataset. Furthermore, the chapter introduces graph data science techniques tailored for fraud detection.

Closing Summary: The Future of Graph Data Science

This concluding chapter envisions the future of graph data science. It emphasizes the role of graph technology in deriving actionable insights and the synergy between knowledge graphs and Large Language Models like GPT for deeper contextual understanding. This forward-looking perspective aims to inspire continued exploration in the field of graph data science.

- Libraries/Tools/Software/Platforms/Programming Languages/Tech:

- Neo4j: Graph database platform

- Python: Programming language for data science

- Cypher: Query language for Neo4j

- Neo4j Bloom: Tool for visualizing graph data

- Graph Embeddings: Techniques for node embeddings and representations

A Note from the Author

Dear readers,

Welcome to this exciting journey into the world of graph data science! I wrote this book to help others understand the concepts of graph data science more quickly, so they can begin to explore and implement these concepts on their own data. This topic has significantly changed my perception of best data practices because so many data use cases are truly graph problems. I am confident that you will quickly understand and embrace this as you read through this book. My goal is to help people like you get up to speed as quickly as possible. Code examples and a GitHub repo with all the code are provided to ensure that you are able to follow along with the examples and get your hands dirty with graph data science straight away!

We will start by introducing concepts of knowledge graphs, which exist all around us, along with the technologies used in this book to communicate and implement graph data science, including Neo4j and Python. Once we have set the foundation, we will dive into practical applications such as constructing knowledge graphs from structured and unstructured data using NLP techniques, implementing graph algorithms, and visualizing graph data to gain insights and knowledge from the data.

Furthermore, we will walk through many graph algorithms with helpful code examples along the way to enable you to follow along and digest the information in a meaningful way. Graph algorithms help us answer routine (yet difficult) questions. For example, "Who is the most 'important' person in this social graph?" or "Which item will this person 'most likely' choose to purchase next?", or "Which of these businesses could be involved in illegal money laundering schemes?"

As you will see, the topic of graph data science stretches across many verticals, which is why I wanted to write this book - to assist data practitioners in their quest to better represent and interpret their data. Let's prepare to embark on this graph data science journey together. All you have to do is follow along and stay curious – your brain will weave a knowledge graph from the contents of this book, delivering wisdom amidst the vast landscape of graph data science!

- Tim Eastridge

Downloading the code bundles and colored images

Please follow the links or scan the QR codes to download the
Code Bundles and Images of the book:

https://github.com/ava-orange-education/Graph-Data-Science-with-Python-and-Neo4j

The code bundles and images of the book are also hosted on
https://rebrand.ly/674a11

In case there's an update to the code, it will be updated on the existing
GitHub repository.

Errata

We take immense pride in our work at **Orange Education Pvt Ltd,** and follow best practices to ensure the accuracy of our content to provide an indulging reading experience to our subscribers. Our readers are our mirrors, and we use their inputs to reflect and improve upon human errors, if any, that may have occurred during the publishing processes involved. To let us maintain the quality and help us reach out to any readers who might be having difficulties due to any unforeseen errors, please write to us at :

errata@orangeava.com

Your support, suggestions, and feedback are highly appreciated.

DID YOU KNOW

Did you know that Orange Education Pvt Ltd offers eBook versions of every book published, with PDF and ePub files available? You can upgrade to the eBook version at **www.orangeava.com** and as a print book customer, you are entitled to a discount on the eBook copy. Get in touch with us at: **info@orangeava.com** for more details.

At **www.orangeava.com**, you can also read a collection of free technical articles, sign up for a range of free newsletters, and receive exclusive discounts and offers on AVA™ Books and eBooks.

PIRACY

If you come across any illegal copies of our works in any form on the internet, we would be grateful if you would provide us with the location address or website name. Please contact us at **info@orangeava.com** with a link to the material.

ARE YOU INTERESTED IN AUTHORING WITH US?

If there is a topic that you have expertise in, and you are interested in either writing or contributing to a book, please write to us at **business@orangeava.com**. We are on a journey to help developers and tech professionals to gain insights on the present technological advancements and innovations happening across the globe and build a community that believes Knowledge is best acquired by sharing and learning with others. Please reach out to us to learn what our audience demands and how you can be part of this educational reform. We also welcome ideas from tech experts and help them build learning and development content for their domains.

REVIEWS

Please leave a review. Once you have read and used this book, why not leave a review on the site that you purchased it from? Potential readers can then see and use your unbiased opinion to make purchase decisions. We at Orange Education would love to know what you think about our products, and our authors can learn from your feedback. Thank you!

For more information about Orange Education, please visit **www.orangeava.com**.

Table of Contents

Introduction to Graph Data Science

Introduction

In this chapter, we will provide an introduction and overview of graph data science as a method to explore contextual relationships in data. We will explore the significance and versatility of graphs in various domains. Our daily lives are full of graphs, from social media to the maps we use to drive to work, to the recommendations provided to us on our favorite TV streaming network.

We will analyze Python and Neo4j as the tools to learn and explore graphs. These tools offer extensive libraries as well as robust community support, which makes them a great choice for the journey of graph data science.

Structure

In this chapter, the following topics will be covered:

- Understanding Graphs, Graph Networks, and their Relevance
- Introduction to Neo4j Graph Database
- Overview of the Importance of Graph Visualizations
- Data Science and Machine Learning
- Introduction to Graph Data Science
- Introduction to the Python Programming Language

Data Science and Machine Learning

Before we jump into the fascinating world of graph data science, it's important to clarify two fundamental terms: *"data science"* and *"machine learning."* While we assume a certain level of familiarity with these concepts, we will guide you along the way.

Data Science is a multidisciplinary field that involves extracting knowledge and insights from data through various techniques such as data mining, data visualization, and statistical analysis. Data science involves the end-to-end process of acquiring, cleaning, transforming, and analyzing data to uncover patterns, make predictions, and drive better decision-making:

Figure 1.1: *Visual of end-to-end data analysis (Source: https://encrypted-tbn0.gstatic.com/images?q=tbn:ANd9GcRXeY_2rpyHpnH9QJYk61usUIQ1NTXrWrQefA&usqp=CAU)*

Machine Learning, on the other hand, is a subset of data science that focuses on developing algorithms and models that enable computers to learn from data and make predictions or take actions without being explicitly programmed. Machine learning algorithms learn from historical data to identify patterns, make predictions, and automate decision-making processes on new, never-before-seen data.

Figure 1.2: *Visual of a computer processing a large amount of historical data and then exporting predictions (Source: https://www.dataversity.net/future-analytics-hype-real/)*

In summary, while the two are often used as synonyms, data science provides the foundation and tools to explore, interpret, and gain insights from data, while machine learning leverages the data to build predictive models and make accurate predictions and/or automated decisions. Together, the two form a powerful combination that drives innovation and enables data-driven solutions.

Defining Graph

While you might first think of a graph as a pie chart or an x and y axis, we refer to a *graph* in this book as something else entirely. In discrete mathematics and graph theory, a graph is a structure that consists of objects or nodes (illustrated as dots in *Figure* 1.3) where pairs of objects or nodes are connected or related in some way. These objects can be referred to as vertices, nodes, or points. In this book, we will refer to these objects as **nodes**.

The connections between the vertices are referred to as edges, relationships, or links (illustrated as lines connecting the dots in *Figure* 1.3). In this book, we will refer to the connections between nodes as relationships.

In Neo4j, data can be stored on both nodes and relationships. We will refer to this data as properties of either the node or **relationship**:

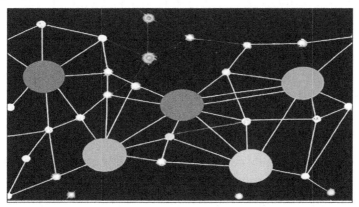

Figure 1.3: *Nodes and Relationships (created using DALL-E)*

The Importance of Graph Structures

Although the concept of graphs may initially seem too "mathematical" or abstract, the truth is that graphs are present in our everyday lives, and we often think in terms of graphs without even realizing it.

Consider your social circle or network of friends. Each person can be represented as a node, while the connections or friendships between individuals can be represented as a relationship. This forms a social graph that helps us understand how people are interconnected and how information flows within our social circles.

In the realm of internet search, graphs are central to search engines like Google. When you enter a search query, Google analyzes the web graph to determine the relevance and importance of different web pages. This enables the search engine to provide you with the most relevant results, considering factors like page popularity, linking patterns, and the overall structure of the web graph.

In transportation and logistics, graphs play a crucial role in route planning and optimization. Road networks can be represented as graphs, with intersections as nodes and roads as relationships. By analyzing this transportation graph, algorithms can calculate the shortest or fastest routes from one location to another, helping us navigate efficiently.

In banking, graphs play a crucial role in detecting potentially suspicious and fraudulent behavior in transaction data. Banks analyze transactional data using graph-based techniques to identify patterns and anomalies that may indicate fraudulent activities. By representing customer accounts, transactions, and their relationships as a graph, banks can detect unusual connections, such as multiple accounts linked to a single individual, unexpected money flows, or patterns resembling known fraud schemes. The graph-based analysis enables banks to proactively monitor and mitigate risks, safeguarding the integrity of financial systems and protecting customers from fraudulent activities. Graphs provide a comprehensive view of transactional networks, empowering banks to stay one step ahead in the constant battle against financial crime.

Graphs are also integral to recommendation systems that suggest products, movies, or music based on our preferences. By analyzing our past interactions, such as purchases, ratings, or clicks, recommendation engines create a personalized graph of our preferences. They then utilize graph-based algorithms to find similar users or items, enabling them to suggest relevant and personalized recommendations.

These examples only scratch the surface of how graphs are utilized in various domains. We will cover each of these topics in depth in this book.

In this chapter, we go beyond just providing you with a knowledge base. Implementing graph data science techniques may initially seem daunting, but don't worry! We will guide you through practical code examples that will not only deepen your understanding but also equip you with the technical abilities required to implement these concepts yourself. While there may be a learning curve, hang tight. This book will provide you with everything you need to succeed. By the end, you will be grateful that you invested the time to read this book, as it will empower you to harness the full potential of graphs and unlock new insights in your data analysis endeavors.

Introducing Neo4j Graph Database

Neo4j is an efficient native graph database. The term *native* means it has been specifically built for handling graph data structures and their associated algorithms and operations. Neo4j has a robust community and documentation. As an open-source platform, it receives maintenance from both internal Neo4j developers as well as a diverse community of external developers.

Neo4j differs from non-native graph databases of the NoSQL or relational types such as MongoDB, Amazon Neptune, SQL Server, and ArangoDB. Furthermore, a native graph database differs from **Resource Description Framework (RDF)** databases, which specialize in data interchange on the Web, such as Virtuoso, Stardog, and others. Lastly, vector databases have increased in popularity since the release of ChatGPT and other more recent **large language models (LLMs).** In this book, we will explore leveraging Neo4j to store vectors and implement similarity searches. However, it is important to note that Neo4j is not considered a vector database per se, unlike Pinecone, Milvus, **FAISS (Facebook AI Similarity Search)**, and others.

To summarize, Neo4j is a very popular graph database because of its scalability, community, and native graph data structure. It's a terrific software choice for datasets that house many connections between data points and where scrutinizing the interconnection of these data points is critical.

Knowledge Graphs

As a data scientist by trade, understanding and appreciating the value of tailoring data to address specific problems at hand is crucial. Whether you are an analyst aiming to extract key insights from the data, a data scientist striving to build accurate predictions, or an executive seeking a cost-effective, flexible, and elegant data design, storing data as a Graph can satisfy both you and your stakeholders' needs.

Within the domain of graph data science, visualizations take center stage as a powerful tool for unraveling the intricacies of complex networks. They allow us to comprehend the subtle relationships within interconnected data and effectively communicate valuable insights. Visual representations play a vital role in bridging the gap between raw data and actionable knowledge:

Figure 1.4: 3D picture of graph (created using DALL-E)

Data storytelling conveys insights, making data relatable and impactful. Graphs enhance communication by visually representing complex information, highlighting patterns, and engaging the audience. Graphs condense data, support the narrative, and enable interactivity for deeper exploration. Effective data storytelling combines narratives with concise and intuitive visualizations to captivate and inform audiences, fostering data-driven decision-making.

In this chapter, we will leverage Bloom for network visualization as well as NetworkX. Bloom is developed and supported by the company Neo4j and offers a terrific platform for data exploration and network analysis. NetworkX is an open-source Python package often used in academia to study the structure, dynamics, and connections of complex networks. NetworkX provides basic visualizations using a Matplotlib backend, but visualizations with this library are fairly limited and may not be suitable for exploring larger networks. In such cases, one may choose to utilize Bloom. There are several vendor tools and open-source options available for visualizing networks as well, which are outside the scope of this book, but are mentioned here:

- **Linkurious**: It is widely used in various fields such as fraud detection, intelligence analysis, and cyber-security.
- **Hume by GraphAware**: Hume is built on top of Neo4j and aims to help organizations derive insights from connected data through visualization,

analysis, and machine learning. Hume allows users to create visualizations that reflect real-world entities and relationships, making it easier to understand complex networks.

- **VizNetwork package in R**: VizNetwork is a package available in the R programming language. It is geared toward the visualization of networks and graphs. VizNetwork allows users to create interactive network graphs and is highly customizable, allowing for different types of nodes, edges, and graph layouts.

- **Gephi**: Gephi is an open-source network visualization and analysis tool. It allows users to explore data through various graphs, interactive visualizations, and statistical reports. Gephi is especially popular in academic and research circles for its extensive capabilities and customizability.

- **D3.js**: D3.js is a JavaScript library for manipulating documents based on data. It can be used to create intricate, interactive graph visualizations in web browsers.

- **Power BI**: Microsoft's Power BI has some network visualization plugins that can be used to incorporate graph data visualizations into broader BI dashboards and reports. However, as of the publication of this book, Power BI's network visualization capabilities are relatively limited. Users are restricted to specific visualizations without much ability to customize visualizations.

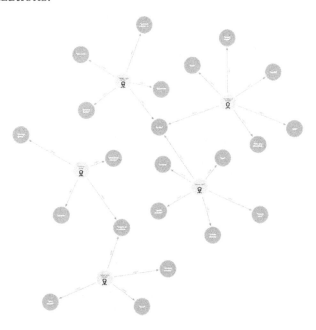

Figure 1.5: *Graph visualization with Neo4j Bloom*

Introducing Python Programming Language

Python is a versatile and easy-to-learn programming language and is often the choice for developers who work with data analysis, aggregation, and manipulation. The company Neo4j supports a Python API driver to connect to the Neo4j database, making for seamless integration. We will cover all the configuration and connection steps in this book.

Furthermore, Python has emerged as one of the most popular programming languages in the data science community in recent years due to its ease of use, extensive libraries, and community support. The language is readable and therefore caters well to professionals without a traditional software engineering background. In data science, Python is widely used for tasks such as statistical analysis, **natural language processing (NLP)**, machine learning, deep learning, and more.

Python is a natural fit to connect to Neo4j due to its relevance in the data science community, Neo4j-supported driver, as well as its extensions to libraries such as NeworkX, which is designed for the creation, manipulation, and analysis of complex graph networks.

It is also worth noting that Neo4j supports drivers for other programming languages such as C#, Java, and Node.js. The terrific Neo4j community has also created community drivers for Go, PHP, Ruby, R, and Scala.

Conclusion

In this chapter, we explored the significance and versatility of graphs in various domains. Graphs are fundamental in our daily lives. The flexibility of this data structure allows for many new opportunities for data storage, data science, and visualization.

Graphs are critical in many domains, including web connections, social interactions, fraud detection, optimal transportation routes, pharmaceuticals, and many more.

We explored why this book covers Python and Neo4j as tools to learn and explore graphs. These tools offer extensive libraries, simplicity, and robust community support, which make them a great choice for the journey of graph data science.

In summary, this chapter lays the foundation for understanding graph data science and its relevance in real-world applications. In the next chapter, we will walk step-by-step through the installation and configuration of Python and Neo4j, so that you can follow along with code examples throughout the book.

Multiple Choice Questions

1. Which of the following best defines the significance of understanding networks?

    a. To analyze social media trends

    b. To map out connections and relationships in various domains

    c. To create visuals for presentations

    d. To increase computer storage

2. What is the primary function of knowledge graphs?

    a. Displaying statistical data

    b. Linking interconnected data and concepts

    c. Creating 3D graphics

    d. Organizing data in tables

3. Why is Python frequently chosen for graph-related tasks?

    a. It's the newest programming language

    b. It has a snake logo

    c. It offers a range of libraries and tools suitable for graph operations

    d. It's only for web development

4. What is Neo4j primarily used for?

    a. Storing relational database tables

    b. Processing large text files

    c. Storing and querying graph data

    d. Designing website interfaces

5. Why are graph visualizations crucial in the context of networks and graphs?

    a. They make data colorful and vibrant

    b. They help spot patterns and relationships easily

    c. They are necessary for printing

    d. They increase the speed of the database

Answers

1. b

2. b

3. c

4. c

5. b

## CHAPTER 2

Getting Started with Python and Neo4j

Introduction

Python and Neo4j are both terrific tools for graph data science. Each offers powerful tools and frameworks to analyze interconnected data. In theory, it is possible to implement end-to-end graph data science with either Python or Neo4j individually. However, in practice, it is much simpler to leverage both tools together to maximize the value of each tool.

Python has become one of the most popular programming languages in the data science community due to its rich ecosystem of libraries and packages, allowing all users to leverage the incredible work of others and jumpstart their analysis. Python comes with several **integrated development environments (IDEs)** that facilitate code visualization, allowing users not only to view and debug their code but also to create graphs, charts, and various other visual representations of data.

Neo4j is a highly efficient native graph database well-known for its ability to manage complex data relationships effectively. It is the most popular and prominent graph database, which means the community and documentation are mature and well-established. The vibrant community of developers sets Neo4j apart. Being an open-source platform, it benefits from contributions from these developers. This consolidation of a strong community and efficient speed makes Neo4j a great choice in the realm of graph databases.

Structure

In this chapter, the following topics will be covered:

- Installation Process of Python
- Understanding Cypher Query Language
- Installation Process of Neo4j
- Understanding the Interfaces
- Connecting to the Neo4j Database from Python
- Code Examples for Better Comprehension

Installing and Setting Up Python and Neo4j

Now, we will walk through the step-by-step process of installing and setting up Python and Neo4j on your system. As we discussed previously, Python is a versatile programming language widely used in data science, while Neo4j is a powerful graph database that enables efficient management and analysis of interconnected data. This guide will assist you in unleashing the power and potential of these two free software tools for your graph data science projects.

Please note that Neo4j offers a free Neo4j Desktop version as well as a paid Enterprise version of the database. For our demonstrations, we will use version 5.15 of the free Neo4j Desktop database.

Installing Python

Python is available on multiple operating systems, including Linux/Unix, Windows, macOS, Android, iOS, and others such as Raspberry Pi's Raspbian. Python's cross-platform compatibility makes it useful in almost any environment. Here are the steps for installing Python:

1. Navigate to the Anaconda website (https://www.anaconda.com/ download) and download the installer corresponding to your operating system. Anaconda is a popular distribution of Python and R programming aimed to simplify package management and deployment of software required for data science and machine learning projects. Anaconda provides simple and robust package management, pre-installed libraries, and environment management. It is a great choice for both novice and

experienced data enthusiasts, as it streamlines the setup and management of the tools and libraries required for analytics.

2. Follow the on-screen instructions and run the downloaded installer. Choose an installation path and select the options to fit your needs.

3. Open the Anaconda Navigator, a **graphical user interface (GUI)** that provides access to Python packages, tools, and integrated development environments such as **Jupyter Notebook**, as shown in the following figure:

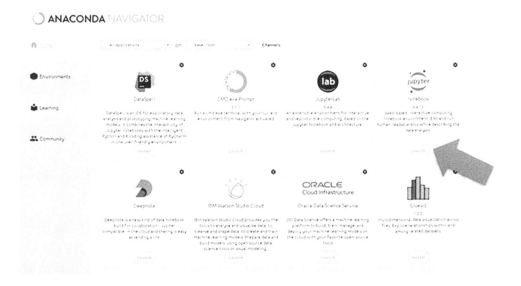

Figure 2.1: *Anaconda application home screen*

"Hello-World" Example with Python

"Hello World" is a programming practice employed to verify the functionality of programming languages and ensure everything has been installed properly.

Once you have the Anaconda Navigator dashboard open, click **Launch** under Jupyter Notebook. Next, select the **New** button and select **Python 3** (or whichever version of Python you have installed on your machine). This will open a new Jupyter Notebook:

Figure 2.2: *Creating a Jupyter Notebook*

The new Jupyter Notebook will appear something like this:

Figure 2.3: *New Jupyter Notebook Interface*

Next, type ``**`print('Hello World!')`**`` *into the blank cell and press CTRL + Enter* to execute the selected cell. *Shift + Enter* will run the current cell and then automatically move to the next cell. Please note that we are using Windows for our demonstration in this book. On a macOS, the command would be *Command + Enter.*

Alternatively, you can click the `Run` button in the toolbar at the top of the notebook:

Figure 2.4: *Command executed in Jupyter Notebook*

Executing Python Code Using Common Libraries

When you use Python through the Anaconda distribution, you have several pre-loaded packages ready to be utilized. These packages encompass a wide range of functionalities, and we will dive into a few of the most common packages.

In the following code block, we will load packages in the first five lines, and then create a pandas dataframe. Next, we will use Matplotlib to plot the data and perform a simple linear regression with scikit-learn to generate a line of best fit for the dataset. For context, here are a few descriptions:

- **pandas**: A Python library used for data manipulation and analysis, useful for working with structured data in rows and columns, handling missing data, and performing other useful transformations and analysis.
- **Matplotlib**: A plotting library with animations, interactive visualizations, and other fundamental tools for scientific visualization.
- **scikit-learn**: A Python library for machine learning with algorithms for classification, regression, and more. It is known for its simplicity and ease of use.
- **"Best Fit" in a dataset**: In the context of machine learning, "*best-fit*" refers to a model or a line that best represents the relationship between variables. For instance, in linear regression, a best-fit line is a straight line that minimizes the distance between data points.

```python
import numpy as np

import pandas as pd

import matplotlib.pyplot as plt

from sklearn.linear_model import LinearRegression

from scipy import stats


# Creating a Pandas DataFrame

data = {'Column1': [1, 2, 3, 4, 5], 'Column2': [6, 7, 8, 9, 10]}

df = pd.DataFrame(data)


# Plotting the data points from the DataFrame using Matplotlib

plt.scatter(df['Column1'], df['Column2'], color='red', label='Data Points')
```

```
# Plotting the line using Matplotlib
plt.plot(df['Column1'], df['Column2'], label='Line of Best Fit')

# Adding labels and title
plt.xlabel('Column1')
plt.ylabel('Column2')
plt.title('Simple Plot with Data Points and Line of Best Fit')
plt.legend()

# Display the plot
plt.show()

# Performing a simple linear regression using scikit-learn
X = df['Column1'].values.reshape(-1, 1)
y = df['Column2'].values
model = LinearRegression().fit(X, y)

# Using SciPy to perform a simple t-test
t_statistic, p_value = stats.ttest_ind(df['Column1'], df['Col-
umn2'])
print("t-statistic:", t_statistic, "p-value:", p_value)
```

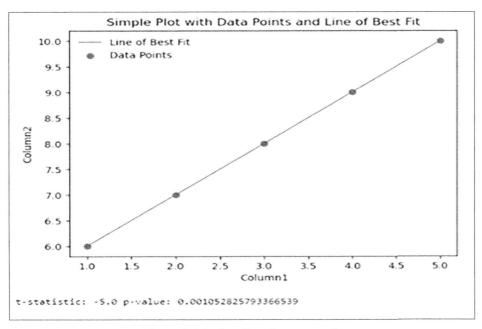

Figure 2.5: *Python line chart example*

In the preceding figure, we use the Matplotlib library to visualize the line of best fit, which minimizes the distances between the red data points. This is a common machine learning technique to represent the distances between existing data points to predict new and unseen data.

Incorporating New Libraries Using Conda

As mentioned previously, utilizing Anaconda as your Python distribution comes with several advantages, including the package manager, Conda. Conda is a powerful package manager with a comprehensive library of over 7500 data science and machine learning libraries out of the box.

We will use the library xgboost in the next section to illustrate advanced machine learning on a popular data science dataset. However, xgboost does not come pre-installed with Anaconda. Therefore, we will need to use the Conda package manager to install this library. If you try to load the xgboost package before you install it with Conda, then you will see an error message, as shown in the following figure:

```
In [4]: import xgboost as xgb

ModuleNotFoundError                       Traceback (most recent call last)
~\AppData\Local\Temp\ipykernel_10108\591698938.py in <module>
----> 1 import xgboost as xgb

ModuleNotFoundError: No module named 'xgboost'
```

Figure 2.6: *Example error message in loading a Python package*

Let's use Conda to install this package:

```
In [5]: conda install xgboost

Collecting package metadata (current_repodata.json): ...working... done
Solving environment: ...working... done
```

Figure 2.7: *Python package installation*

Next, let's install the libraries needed later to connect to the Neo4j database via an API from Python and load these libraries into our workspace:

```
conda install neo4j
```

```
conda install graphdatascience
```

```
import xgboost as xgb
from neo4j import GraphDatabase
from graphdatascience import GraphDataScience
```

Figure 2.8: *Install and loaded necessary Python packages*

Introduction to Cypher in Neo4j

Cypher is a query language designed for working with graph databases, particularly Neo4j. In the same way that relational databases use SQL, the graph database uses Cypher. It is used to create, update, and retrieve data from a graph database. Its structure is intuitive and allows for pattern matching that is clear and expressive.

For example, the MATCH statement is used to retrieve data. A query that starts with `MATCH (p:Person)` will search all person nodes in the database. We can then use the WHERE clause to specify which persons to retrieve. Finally, we can use the RETURN statement to indicate which elements to return in the result set.

For beginners in the world of graph databases and Neo4j, mastering Cypher is an important step to effectively query and analyze graph data. We will continue to use Cypher throughout this book to help readers understand and master the query language.

Installing GDS and APOC Plugins

The **Graph Data Science (GDS)** library and the **Awesome Procedures on Cypher (APOC)** are two plugins that dramatically improve the capabilities of the Neo4j database. We will need to install these plugins to perform advanced graph algorithms, operations, and connection to Python via the GDS driver.

The company Neo4j supports the GDS library, which includes 50+ data science algorithms.

APOC is a library containing a collection of user-defined procedures and functions that complement and extend the capabilities of Neo4j. The APOC library is used for many tasks, such as:

- Data integration of various data sources such as JSON or XML
- Utility functions such as batch processing and generating UUIDs
- Execute Cypher queries in parallel
- Performance monitoring tools and execution plans
- Geospatial functions such as calculating the distance between two coordinates
- Time series analysis

You do not need to worry about installing these Plugins if you are only using Aura. If you are using Neo4j Desktop, then you will need to follow these steps:

1. Click the gray area to the left of the **Start** button to select the database .

2. Click the **Plugins** tab.

3. Click **Install** under both the APOC as well as GDS dropdowns.

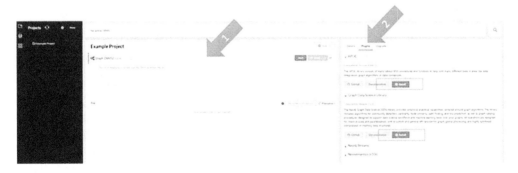

Figure 2.9: *Steps to install Plugins on Neo4j Desktop*

Installing and Setting Up the Neo4j Database

Neo4j is renowned for its ability to manage, query, and analyze data with complex relationships and interconnected elements. Next, we will guide you through the setup required to connect Python to both the free Neo4j Desktop as well as the fully managed Aura Cloud database, which offers a free, small-sized server for experimentation.

Neo4j Desktop is a convenient local development environment optimal for those looking to explore the capabilities of Neo4j without working with cloud configurations or inert connectivity. It's beneficial for small teams and individuals working on a prototype or learning how to use graph databases. Neo4j Desktop allows developers to have multiple graph instances and projects running at the same time. Furthermore, its user-friendly interface makes it easier to manage databases and install plugins. Lastly, data privacy is inherently more controlled as the data resides on the local machine.

Neo4j Aura, on the other hand, is a cloud-based, fully managed database-as-a-service, which is ideal for production deployments and scaling. Developers can focus on building applications without the overhead concerns of maintenance tasks and operational overhead associated with running a database. Aura provides automated backups, high availability, and seamless scalability; however, this comes at a financial cost. Not to worry, in this book, we will tinker with the free version of Aura.

Neo4j Desktop Installation on Local Machine

Neo4j offers several ways to leverage its graph database software. Navigate to this link (https://neo4j.com/download-center/#desktop) for options to install the Neo4j Desktop to your local machine:

Once installed, click the **Add** button to create a new database within your project:

Figure 2.10: *Add a new database within your project*

Next, click **Start** to start your database:

Figure 2.11: *Start the Neo4j Desktop database*

Once the database is running, click the dropdown next to **Open** and choose **Neo4j Browser**. We will start with this interface as a means to interact with some example data:

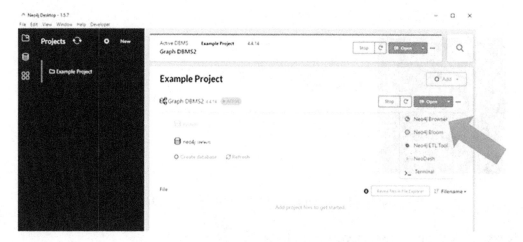

Figure 2.12: *Open the Neo4j Browser*

Once the Neo4j Browser is open, type '`:play movies`' in the console and then press Enter to execute this line of code:

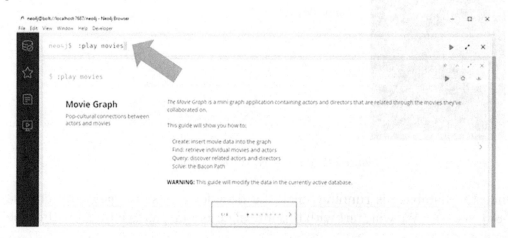

Figure 2.13: *Run command in Neo4j Browser for the Movies tutorial*

You will see a slider box with 1/8 tabs, as illustrated above. This tutorial is provided to help beginners understand how to use Neo4j. Navigate to the second page, as shown in *Figure 2.14*, click the `Play` button, and you will see your first graph appear in Neo4j! This is a graph where the nodes represent People and Movies, and the relationships indicate whether the people `ACTED_IN`, `PRODUCED`, or `DIRECTED` the movie:

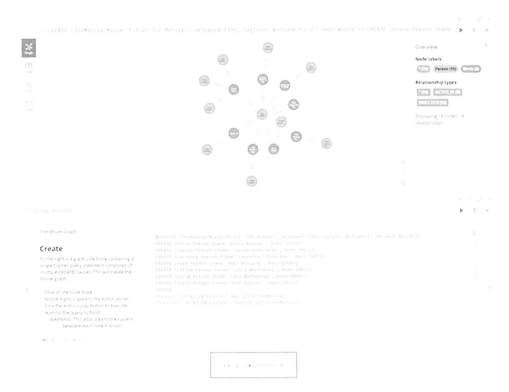

Figure 2.14: *Neo4j Browser movie data visualization*

Introduction to Neo4j Aura Database

Another method to access Neo4j is to use the managed cloud environment, Aura. To connect, navigate to the Neo4j Aura website and sign up for an account. Once you are logged in, click "New Instance." Be sure to save a copy of the one-time generated password. Neo4j will not ask for a credit card, so do not worry about paying to use the free database. If you decide to scale up your application later, you can increase the size of your instance and place a credit card on file at that time.

For more information, please visit https://neo4j.com/cloud/platform/aura-graph-database/

Once the instance has been created, click **Query**:

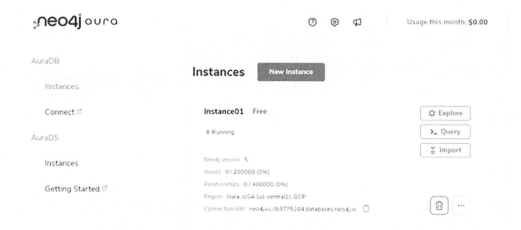

Figure 2.15: *Open Neo4j Browser to query the new Aura database*

Once the Neo4j Browser is loaded, you can run the same '`:play movies`' in the console and then press '*Enter*' to execute this line of code:

Figure 2.16: *Run the Play Movies example*

From here, you can follow the aforementioned steps to create your first graph in the Aura database environment!

Connecting Python to Neo4j

Connecting Python to Neo4j enables developers to interact with the Neo4j graph database using Python scripts. Once a connection has been established between Python and Neo4j, you can create, read, update, and delete nodes and relationships in the Neo4j database efficiently and easily. We will first connect to the database and then cover these additional functionalities in later chapters.

Connecting to Neo4j Desktop uses a local connection. (If you are using the Aura DB, then there will be a URI connection string, which will be covered later.) The port number in Neo4j Desktop, which is essential for the connection, can be found by launching the Neo4j Browser. Open the Neo4j Browser and look at the top left corner:

Figure 2.17: Local host connection to Neo4j Browser

Next, run the following code to connect to Neo4j. In this code snippet, first load all the necessary libraries. Second, enter the URI string, username, and password. Lastly, use the `GraphDataScience` function to create an API connection between Python and Neo4j:

Connect to Neo4j

```python
from neo4j import GraphDatabase
from graphdatascience import GraphDataScience
import pandas as pd

uri = "bolt://localhost:7687" # CHANGE TO YOUR PORT NUMBER
user = "neo4j"
password = "neo4j12345"       # CHANGE PASSWORD

gds = GraphDataScience(uri, auth=(user,password))
gds.set_database("neo4j")

gds.run_cypher("""

MATCH (n:Person)
RETURN n.name as Name
LIMIT 5

""")
```

	Name
0	Keanu Reeves
1	Carrie-Anne Moss
2	Laurence Fishburne
3	Hugo Weaving
4	Lilly Wachowski

Figure 2.18: Connect to Neo4j using Python API

In the URI string, we use the Bolt protocol to communicate with Neo4j. This is a binary protocol, which means it is optimized for transmitting graph data. Bolt is faster in terms of data transfer compared to HTTP/HTTPS. Additionally, Bolt supports TLS encryption out of the box to ensure secure data transmission.

On-Premise or Cloud Configurations

While the topic of on-premises and specialized cloud Neo4j configurations is outside the scope of this book, it is important to mention that Neo4j offers robust documentation on this topic. Cloud computing and large-scale clusters of on-premises servers are very common in production environments, and system administrators typically handle various components such as:

- System Installation and Setup
- Memory Configuration
- Security Configuration
- Performance Tuning
- Backup and Recovery
- Network Configuration
- Logs and Monitoring

If you are a system administrator and would like to learn more about Neo4j in the cloud, refer to the following documentation link. If you are installing an on-premise Linux server, you can also find documentation at the same link: https://neo4j.com/developer/guide-cloud-deployment/

Conclusion

Congratulations! You have successfully installed Python and Neo4j, created your first Neo4j graph model, and connected your Python environment to the Neo4j database. In this chapter, we discussed how to install Python and Neo4j, so that you can bolster your graph data science journey at a rapid pace. We walked through the step-by-step process of installing Python by leveraging the Anaconda distribution, introduction to the Cypher query language, and the installation of the Neo4j database.

In the next chapter, we will begin our analytics within the Neo4j database and then connect Python to Neo4j to further bolster our analysis in the subsequent chapter.

## CHAPTER 3

Importing Data into the Neo4j Graph Database

Introduction

In a world of ever-expanding data and increasingly complex relationships between data points, graph databases have emerged as a powerful method to model, store, and query interconnected data in an efficient and meaningful manner. Neo4j, at the forefront of the graph data revolution, offers a complementary product complete with various analytics methods out of the box, enabling you to harness the full potential of your data.

In this chapter, we take a closer look at the Neo4j database with its flexible and scalable design, which facilitates queries to quickly analyze these relationships in the data. You will gain a strong understanding of the fundamental mechanics of Neo4j.

The code examples are included, and you are encouraged to actively engage with the code in this chapter. This hands-on approach will help facilitate a deeper understanding of each concept discussed in this chapter.

Structure

In this chapter, we will cover the following topics:

- Understanding the differences between graph databases and traditional relational databases
- Features and advantages of the Neo4j graph database
- Graph database terminology
- Introduction to the Neo4j Cypher query language
- Importing data into Neo4j

Understanding the Neo4j Graph Database

Neo4j is a highly flexible and scalable graph database. Unlike traditional relational databases, which use tables to store data, graph databases like Neo4j use graph structures with nodes, edges, and properties to represent and store data.

Neo4j is an open-source graph database, implemented using Java. The architecture of Neo4j is built from the ground up and designed to manage graphs with these key aspects:

- **Native Graph Storage**: This means that nodes and relationships are stored near each other under the hood, resulting in faster retrieval times.

- **Index-Free Adjacency**: Neo4j stores the data with index-free adjacency, which means that nodes physically point to their connected nodes in storage. This eliminates the need for index lookups and large table scans, which significantly speeds up query performance.

- **Scalability**: Neo4j is highly scalable and can handle very large datasets as well as complex relationships between data points.

- **ACID Transactions**: ACID (**Atomicity, Consistency, Isolation, Durability**) properties are fundamental database transaction attributes that guarantee the reliability of data in a database-managed system:

  o **Atomicity** ensures that each transaction is treated as an indivisible, single unit where, if any step fails, then none of the changes are committed, preventing partial updates and/or corrupted data. This is extremely important in industries such as Finance or E-commerce where each individual unit is extremely important, and the accuracy of the transaction must be 100% guaranteed.

  o **Consistency** of a transaction means the transaction is guaranteed to remain consistent when transferring from one state to another. This is very important in industries like Healthcare where patient records must remain consistent across records.

  o **Isolation** enables the transaction to occur in a manner that makes them appear as if they were processed sequentially which prevents one transaction from affecting the data used by another transaction. This is important in industries like Airline Reservations or Stock Trading where multiple customers are attempting to claim resources simultaneously. Isolation ensures these transactions do not interfere with one another and that the transaction is executed accurately.

  o **Durability** guarantees the committed transaction will remain consistent even in the event of server failure or power outage. This is important in Disaster Recovery situations to ensure critical data is not lost.

Features and Advantages of Neo4j for Graph Data Science

Neo4j offers many graph algorithms out-of-the-box, which enables you to run 'In-Database Analytics.' This ability to run algorithms in your database without porting your data to another analytics environment running Python or SAS will be more efficient, saving you money by reducing complexities in your architecture as well as reducing data redundancy and server energy expenses.

Furthermore, Neo4j offers a flexible schema. Unlike traditional relational databases, which require a rigid schema, Neo4j allows for an adaptable data model which can mold and be shaped over time. This enables you to evolve your data store and refactor your schema as new data sources emerge. Complex data models can be implemented without the need for extensive planning and redesign, which results in faster development cycles.

The Cypher Query Language is a unique, intuitive query language developed by Neo4j to make it simple to work with graph data. The language is easily readable and mirrors the way we visualize graphs. Cypher allows the user to generate complex, multi-hop queries with pattern matching in a simple 2-3 lines of code. In comparison, a relational database query to accomplish the same task could be dozens of lines of code involving multiple sub-queries and table joins, and would run more slowly compared to the Cypher query in Neo4j.

To summarize, Neo4j is faster and easier to use for many of your interconnected data needs, which saves you time and money. Not only can you start building your data more quickly, but you can also query your data more efficiently as well. In deciding to switch to a graph database like Neo4j, you need to determine the *right tool for the job*. If you are working with data containing many iterations of connections to other data points, then Neo4j might be the right tool for you.

Graph Database Terminology and Concepts

As we jump into the graph databases, it is essential to familiarize yourself with the fundamental terminology. Understanding these foundational elements will provide you with the knowledge to succeed with graph databases. Sometimes, it is easiest to imagine a graph database as a complex spider web where each data point is connected to other data points. Graph databases help solve the valuable CTO's million-dollar (or billion-dollar) question of how we connect the dots to draw data insights.

Nodes are the '**dots**' in terms of connecting the dots. Nodes are much like the individual *records* in a database (or *rows* in an Excel spreadsheet). Each node can be represented by a **Label** such as 'Movie' or 'Actor.' Labels can be thought of as the *columns* of a table in relational data.

Relationships connect the nodes (or dots in the connecting-the-dots analogy). Relationships are directed and always have a start and end node and represent the associates between nodes. For example, you may have nodes of 'Individuals' and you can connect these individuals with the relationship of 'FRIEND_OF' to illustrate that one individual is a friend of another individual.

Properties are additional data elements stored on the node. For example, you may have a label of an individual with properties such as Name, Date of Birth, and Unique ID. Properties can be thought of as additional columns in a relational database that help describe each record/row in the data.

Relationship Properties are data elements stored in the relationship. For example, you may have a relationship of 'FRIEND_OF' between two individuals and you may want to enrich this relationship with additional attributes such as Timestamp of Most Recent Interaction, Count of Messages Between Individuals, and Derived Weight / Score of Friendship.

Graph Traversal is the process of moving between nodes via relationships. This is a fundamental operation in querying graph databases due to the nature of how graph databases store connections. One of the terms frequently associated with graph traversal is the "**number of hops**." A hop in this context refers to the transition from one node to another node via a relationship. For example, in a social network graph, if Mitch is friends with Carl, and Carl is friends with Nathan, moving from Mitch to Carl would be one hop. Similarly, moving from Mitch to Nathan would be two hops. The number of hops can be used as a measure of closeness between nodes in a graph.

"**Degrees of separation**" is a concept that closely parallels the idea of "number of hops." Degrees of separation is a term often used in social networks to describe the distance between two points based on relationships or the minimum number of connections needed for a chain of relationships. For example, in the previous example with Mitch, Carl, and Nathan, Mitch and Nathan are said to be two degrees of separation apart.

Introduction to Cypher Query Language

Cypher is the query language developed by Neo4j to provide an intuitive way of working with graph data. Cypher is declarative by nature, which allows you to describe what you are looking to find and not have to explicitly write how to find it. It is often compared to SQL for relational databases in so far as it's an intuitive way to send a request to the database for the data you need. Cypher is known for its simplicity as a means to efficiently query, transform, and extract data.

Cypher was designed with a straightforward graph pattern matching syntax, making the queries readable and easy to understand. Let's break down the following query:

1. Use the word '**MATCH**' to select the pattern we are looking to return.

2. Create a variable, **i1**, to specify the Label of the first node we want to match in our query. There are often multiple Labels in your databases, such as 'Individual', 'Address', and 'Phone', which can be used to distinguish between various entities.

3. Create the variable, r, to specify the type of relationship we want to use to match the two nodes in our query. In this case, we are looking to return the 'FRIENDS_OF' relationship.

4. Incorporate the 'WHERE' clause to specify the specific conditions that must be fulfilled by the nodes and relationships being queried. In this case, the individual, i1, must have a property, 'name,' equal to the value of 'Mitch.'

5. Use the 'RETURN' clause to dictate the elements to be returned. The asterisk will instruct the query to return the entire set of matched elements. Rather than use the asterisk, you could also write "RETURN i1, r, i2" to accomplish the same result:

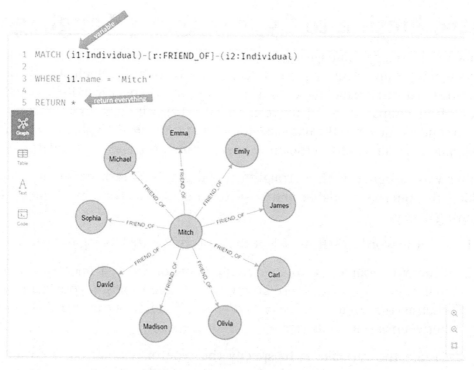

Figure 3.1: *Syntax of a Cypher Query*

When we talk about graph databases, it's not just the graphical representations that are valuable but also the ability to retrieve data in a structured, tabular format. Cypher can efficiently return data as a relational table. In the following example, we illustrate Cypher's ability to return the same data as above, but in tabular, relational form:

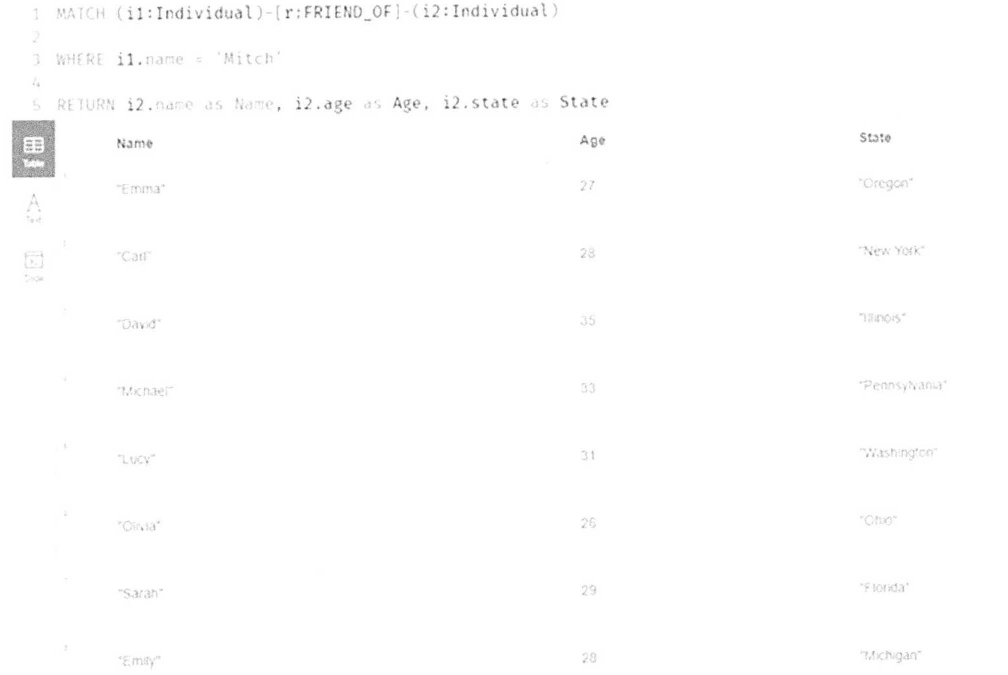

```
1  MATCH (i1:Individual)-[r:FRIEND_OF]-(i2:Individual)
2
3  WHERE i1.name = 'Mitch'
4
5  RETURN i2.name as Name, i2.age as Age, i2.state as State
```

Name	Age	State
"Emma"	27	"Oregon"
"Carl"	28	"New York"
"David"	35	"Illinois"
"Michael"	33	"Pennsylvania"
"Lucy"	31	"Washington"
"Olivia"	26	"Ohio"
"Sarah"	29	"Florida"
"Emily"	28	"Michigan"

Figure 3.2: *Relational, tabular data output from a Cypher query*

Data Import

Data import is the foundational step of all data analytics processes bridging data sources into a unified platform for analysis. Data import is pivotal as it provides the data needed for analysis and impacts the quality and accuracy of the derived insights. Effective data import ensures the subsequent steps of data handling and transformation and pattern detection yield meaningful results.

Data Transformations and Preprocessing in Neo4j

Transforming data (aka preprocessing) is a critical step before ingesting data into Neo4j. Graph databases thrive on connected data and the quality of the insights you can gain depends on how well the data is connected and structured.

Extract, Transform, and Load (ETL) is the process of extracting data from various sources, transforming it into a structured format, and loading it into the target data store or database. In the context of Neo4j, ETL is important as it enables us to efficiently store, manage, and manipulate graph data.

We have included a Python script that executes the ETL procedures used to create the datasets used in this chapter. While we will not go through each step, we encourage you to take a look at this file and familiarize yourself with the various methods you can use to arrange files in the format you need for optimal graph import performance.

In general, it is best practice to create files of nodes and relationships in **Comma Separated Values (CSV)** format. CSV files are plain text files that use commas to separate values, which makes them versatile and compatible with many processing tools. For those of you accustomed to using Excel, you may have encountered Excel has a row limit which can be a constraint when working with large files. CSV files, on the other hand, do not have this limitation. By utilizing CSV files for nodes and relationship files, you can handle much larger datasets. Lastly, CSV files are often more efficient in terms of processing time and memory usage compared to other storage methods, which is an advantage when importing into a graph database like Neo4j.

Creating Data with Cypher

As we mentioned before, one method to load data into Neo4j is through direct transactions with Cypher. In the following code , you can see that we create new nodes with the label 'Individual' and connect these individuals with the relationship, `FRIEND_OF.'

```
```

CREATE (mitch:Individual {name: 'Mitch'});

CREATE (carl:Individual {name: 'Carl'}),
       (nathan:Individual {name: 'Nathan'}),
       (sophia:Individual {name: 'Sophia'}),
       (emma:Individual {name: 'Emma'}),
       (olivia:Individual {name: 'Olivia'}),
       (james:Individual {name: 'James'}),
       (michael:Individual {name: 'Michael'}),
       (emily:Individual {name: 'Emily'}),
       (madison:Individual {name: 'Madison'}),
```
```

```
(david:Individual {name: 'David'}),


(mitch)-[:FRIEND_OF]->(carl),
(mitch)-[:FRIEND_OF]->(sophia),
(mitch)-[:FRIEND_OF]->(emma),
(mitch)-[:FRIEND_OF]->(olivia),
(mitch)-[:FRIEND_OF]->(james),
(mitch)-[:FRIEND_OF]->(michael),
(mitch)-[:FRIEND_OF]->(emily),
(mitch)-[:FRIEND_OF]->(madison),
(mitch)-[:FRIEND_OF]->(david),


(carl)-[:FRIEND_OF]->(nathan);
```
```

While this method of import is straightforward, intuitive, and gets the job done quickly, this method is not feasible for large data files. In the following sections, we will explore some of the most common methods to import large-scale data into Neo4j.

# Importing Data into Neo4j Aura

Neo4j Aura can be one of the most convenient and easiest-to-learn approaches for importing data into Neo4j. Aura comes with a 'Data Importer tool.'

In this section, we will walk you through the process of importing data into Neo4j Aura, step by step, and help you understand the fundamentals while also learning the Neo4j Aura environment.

We will start by loading the Recipe datasets in the code files for this chapter. The free version of Aura has a limit of 200,000 nodes and 400,000 relationships. Therefore, we will utilize the 'Sample_' files of ingredients and recipes to illustrate the load process and focus on the full data load onto Neo4j Desktop in a later section.
```

1. First, click the **Import** button in Aura:

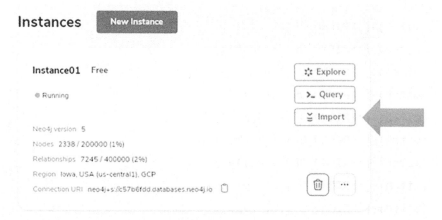

Figure 3.3: *Import Data in Aura DB*

2. From here, you can either click the dropdown and select '**Open model (with data)**' and choose the file '**Aura-Recipe-data-importer.zip**' from the reference folder for the chapter or recreate the following data model using the sample files in the reference folder.

    The data model for this dataset is straightforward: a recipe uses multiple ingredients. Those ingredients are shared across multiple recipes. Also, the '**Recipe**' node has the directions for each recipe as well as a URL to allow you to find the original recipe online:

Figure 3.4: *Create a data model for import in Aura DB*

3. Once you click the '**Recipe**' node, the '**Mapping Details**' will appear on the right side of your screen. From here, you can select all the properties you would like to include from the CSV file:

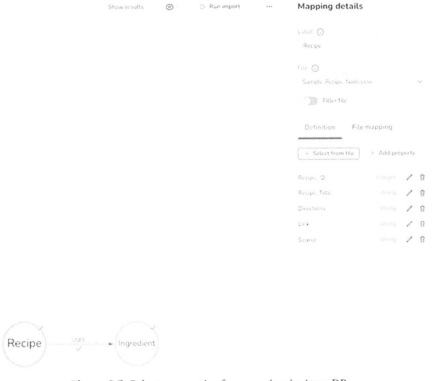

Figure 3.5: *Select properties for mapping in Aura DB*

4. Next, click on the relationship 'USES' to specify the unique IDs to connect the nodes. In this example, we have a 'Recipe_ID', which is a unique numerical ID for each Recipe. Similarly, we have the 'Ingredient_ID' to specify each unique Ingredient.

You will notice the terms 'From' and 'To', which identify the direction of the relationship between nodes. These terms can alternatively be thought of as '**Source**' and '**Target**', where '**Source**' corresponds to the '**From**' and represents the starting point of the relationship, whereas '**Target**' aligns with the 'To' and denotes the endpoint of the relationship:

Figure 3.6: *Create relationship mapping in Aura DB*

5. Once you have the data model formatted correctly and you see the green check marks above the nodes and relationships, then click the `Run Import` button:

Figure 3.7: *Confirmation message of data import in Aura DB*

6. After the import has been completed successfully, let's open Neo4j Bloom to visualize the data! Click the '`Explore`' button on the Aura homepage:

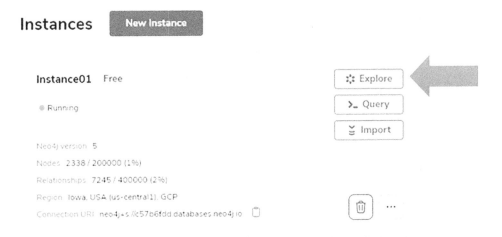

Figure 3.8: *Explore the Aura DB with Bloom*

7.   We will explain how to format Neo4j Bloom later in this book. For now, navigate to the top left of Bloom and select '**neo4j**' to go back to the Perspectives page. We will import a Bloom perspective created for you and save it in the reference material for this chapter:

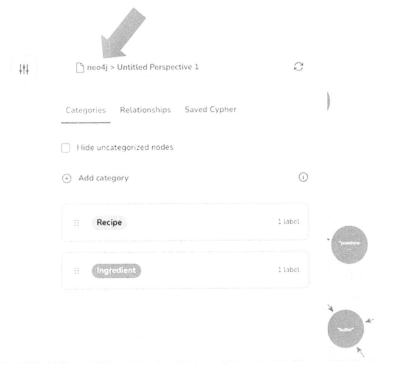

Figure 3.9: *Navigate back to the Bloom perspectives*

8. From here, you will need to first click '**Import**' and then select the '`Bloom_Recipe_Perspective.json`' file.

9. Secondly, select the box '`Bloom_Recipe_Perspective`' to open the Bloom perspective:

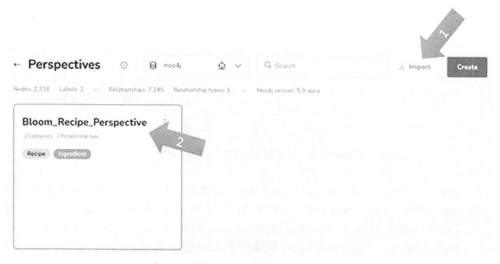

Figure 3.10: *Import Bloom Perspective*

10. Type '`Return Recipe Graph`' in the search bar, then click *Enter*:

Figure 3.11: *Run the Return Recipe Graph command in Bloom*

11. You will see the following network appear. If you double-click on one of the recipes, you will see all the directions involved in creating the recipe.

As you can see, "butter" and "`cream of mushroom soup`" are two shared ingredients in the selected recipes. We will dive deeper into shared connections, commonly used ingredients, and graph data science algorithms to explore this data in more detail in later chapters of this book:

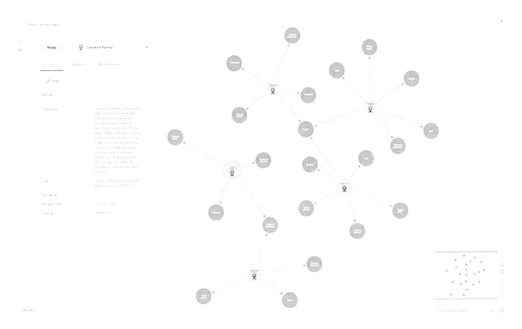

Figure 3.12: *Visual of the recipe graph in Bloom*

Importing Data into Neo4j Desktop with Admin Import

The Neo4j Admin Import tool is a command-line utility that comes bundled with Neo4j Desktop, Neo4j Server, and Neo4j Enterprise. It is designed to facilitate the high-performance import of large volumes of data into a Neo4j database. This is the fastest method to import data into Neo4j because it bypasses the transaction layer, which requires logging, thereby reducing overhead and especially beneficial when you need to load a substantial volume of new data.

While there are many advantages to using Admin Import, it's important to acknowledge certain limitations and prerequisites associated with the tool. The tool does not permit updates or modifications to existing data in the database. Its utility is confined to loading new data. Furthermore, the setup process for Admin Import CSV files is marginally more complicated compared to other import methods. Lastly, one must have administrative privileges to execute the Admin Import tool from the command line terminal. Therefore, this may pose a constraint in certain environments where administrative access is restricted. It is important to balance the benefits with these considerations in deciding when and how to effectively employ the Admin Import tool.

Other import methods, such as Apache Spark, are currently required to log each transaction to Neo4j. Therefore, even though Spark writes the data in parallel, it is much slower to import the data compared to Admin Import. Anecdotally, large Neo4j databases with more than **1 billion** nodes and relationships have been observed to take approximately 48 hours to load with Spark. The Admin Import's ability to dump the data into the database reduced the load time from 48 hours to **under 1 hour**.

Before you begin with Admin Import, follow these steps:

1. Check the documentation for your operating system.

2. Check your version of Neo4j. If you are using version 4 rather than version 5, then the syntax may appear different than it appears in this book.

Here are the steps to run Admin Import:

1. Rename CSV headers to comply with the Admin Import standards. For more information, refer to the following documentation:

    a. https://neo4j.com/docs/operations-manual/current/tutorial/neo4j-admin-import/

    b. https://neo4j.com/docs/operations-manual/current/tools/neo4j-admin/neo4j-admin-import/#import-tool-header-format

2. Move the CSV files to the Neo4j Import folder.

3. Open the Terminal and run the neo4j-admin script.

4. *Optionally*, from the Terminal, update the folder permissions for the new database.

5. Run the 'CREATE DATABASE <databaseName>' command from the Neo4j Browser.

6. *Optionally*, restart the Neo4j services/server.

The first step of the Admin Import process is to move the CSV files to your Neo4j Import folder. This can be done in Neo4j Desktop by selecting the '**Open Folder**' and then choosing '**Import**' option from the drop-down menu:

Figure 3.13: *Navigate to the Import folder in Neo4j Desktop*

Here's an example command:

```
neo4j-admin database import full --
nodes=import/Sample_Admin_Import_Recipe_Node.csv --
nodes=import/Sample_Admin_Import_Ingredient_Node.csv --
relationships=import/Sample_Admin_Import_Recipe_to_Ingredient_
Relationship.csv --id-type INTEGER recipe
```

```
IMPORT DONE in 4m 5s 765ms.
Imported:
   2366780 nodes
   10457463 relationships
   11426978 properties
Peak memory usage: 1.054GiB
```

Figure 3.14: *Admin Import completion message*

Importing Data into Neo4j with CSVs and Python

One of the most common methods of importing data into Neo4j is through CSV imports with Cypher. We can run these Cypher commands directly from Python. The CSV files must first be saved in the Import folder of your database.

The following code will read the CSV from the Import folder, save the CSV as a variable named row, and then create new Recipe nodes based on each row of the dataset:

```
```

```
LOAD CSV WITH HEADERS FROM 'file:///Fake_Data_FBI_Neo4j.csv' AS row
CALL {
    WITH row
    CREATE (:Person {
        full_name: row.full_name,
        ssn: row.ssn,
        ip_address: row.ip_address,
        email: row.email,
        phone_number: row.phone_number,
        address: row.address,
        suspicious_activity_report: row.suspicious_activity_report,
        FBI_case_number: row.FBI_case_number
    })
}
```

```
```

Note: *When running this command in Python, you may need to use double brackets {{}} in order for the Python interpreter to recognize code within the brackets. You will see this illustrated in the accompanying code for this chapter.*

When using the CSV import method, we recommend using batch import to separate the CSV into smaller chunks as a way to avoid running into memory constraints. You can modify the preceding query to read the CSV into Neo4j in chunks of 1000 rows with this code:

```
```

```
LOAD CSV WITH HEADERS FROM 'file:///Fake_Data_FBI_Neo4j.csv' AS row
WITH row
CALL {
    WITH row
    CREATE (:Person {
        full_name: row.full_name,
        ssn: row.ssn,
        ip_address: row.ip_address,
```

```
        email: row.email,

        phone_number: row.phone_number,

        address: row.address,

        suspicious_activity_report: row.suspicious_activity_report,

        FBI_case_number: row.FBI_case_number

    })
} IN TRANSACTIONS OF 1000 ROWS

;
```
```

It is typically best practice to save each node and each relationship as its own CSV in order to efficiently load the data into the database. However, you are not required to save each node and each relationship as its own file. Instead, you can store the information on the node imported from the CSV and then modify the graph schema with Cypher like this:

```

```
MATCH (p:Person)
WHERE p.phone_number IS NOT NULL
MERGE (ph:Phone {{number: p.phone_number}})
MERGE (p)-[:HAS_PHONE_NUMBER]->(ph)
```
```

This code gathers each Person, creates a new node with the label 'Phone' based on the property from the Person node, and then creates a relationship between the new Phone node and the Person node called 'HAS_PHONE_NUMBER.' You can follow along with the code attached to this chapter to create the full dataset.

To visualize this data, we have included a JSON output of the perspective with this chapter's reference material. Import the Perspective and run 'Return Full Network' to generate the following network image. We will go through the steps required to generate images with Bloom in the next chapter:
```

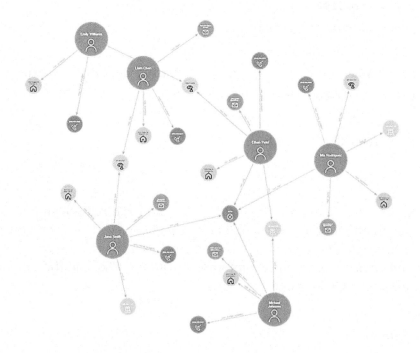

Figure 3.15: *Visual of Mock FBI Data*

Importing Data into Neo4j with Pandas

When dealing with structured data, Pandas is a commonly used library in Python to manipulate and work with data. Importing data into Neo4j from a Pandas dataframe is flexible and convenient. However, this flexibility comes at the expense of speed compared to high-performance data ingestion options such as the Admin Import tool. The primary reason loading data using Pandas (or Spark) is slower is that each transaction must be written to the Transaction logs. The Admin Import tool, on the other hand, does not need to write to the logs and simply bulk imports the data. Having loaded billions of relationships into Neo4j using both a massively parallel Spark method as well as the Admin Import method, we can attest that the Admin Import Tool can be more than 10 times faster.

Let's take a look at loading data using Pandas as this is a flexible method to import data. This method does not require Admin privileges and can therefore be a preferred method for loading ad-hoc, smaller datasets without requiring additional teammates' assistance to import your data.

The GDS library from Neo4j does not currently support data loads directly from Pandas. Therefore, we will create a driver to connect to the database in this section. Please note that when working with drivers and sessions, it is important to close your session when complete. Therefore, we will create and close sessions in the same command to ensure that we do not leave multiple sessions open, which could cause latency for other database users:

```
from neo4j import GraphDatabase
from getpass import getpass

password = getpass()

........

driver = GraphDatabase.driver("bolt://localhost:7687", auth=("neo4j", password))
```

Figure 3.16: Connect to Neo4j with Driver

We are going to use a popular dataset in the data science and machine learning community called 'Iris.' This dataset can be considered the "hello world" dataset of machine learning. It contains 150 samples from each of the three species of the Iris flower: `Setosa`, `Virginica`, and `Versicolor`. The objective is to predict the species of flower based on only the numerical attributes of the flower: `sepal length`, `sepal width`, `petal length`, and `petal width`, all measured in centimeters. The combination of features can help us create a classification machine learning model to distinguish the Species from one another.

We will be taking an innovative approach to convert the tabular data analysis into a graph-based analysis. Graph-based analysis will enable us to harness the power of Neo4j and Neo4j's built-in predictive algorithms to complement our machine learning pipeline. Here is a snapshot of the dataset:

Sepal_Length	Sepal_Width	Petal_Length	Petal_Width	Species
5.1	3.5	1.4	0.2	setosa
4.9	3.0	1.4	0.2	setosa
4.7	3.2	1.3	0.2	setosa
4.6	3.1	1.5	0.2	setosa
5.0	3.6	1.4	0.2	setosa

Figure 3.17: Snapshot of Iris data

Follow along with the provided code to first convert this dataset into a list of dictionaries that we can then import into Neo4j:

```
{'Sepal_Length': 4.9,
 'Sepal_Width': 3.0,
 'Petal_Length': 1.4,
 'Petal_Width': 0.2,
 'Species': 'setosa',
 'Id': '1',
 'Target': 0}
```

Figure 3.18: Iris dataset represented as a list of dictionaries

Once the data is stored as a list of dictionaries, we can import this data into Neo4j using the following Cypher.

The 'UNWIND' clause expands a list of elements into separate rows, effectively taking the data parameter and iterating over each dictionary referred to as a 'row.'

The 'MERGE' clause ensures that a node with the label exists in the database. If a label does not exist, then it creates a new node. If it does exist, then it matches the existing node.

The 'ON CREATE SET' clause is used to set additional properties on the node once the node has been created. We then create a comma-separated list to set each of the columns from the original dataset as properties on the new node:

```
```
with driver.session() as session:
    session.run("""
    UNWIND $data AS row
    MERGE (s:Flower_Record {Row_ID: toInteger(row['Id'])})
    ON CREATE SET s.Target = toInteger(row['Target'])
        , s.Sepal_Length = row['Sepal_Length']
        , s.Sepal_Width = row['Sepal_Width']
        , s.Petal_Length = row['Petal_Length']
        , s.Petal_Width = row['Petal_Width']
        , s.Species   = row['Species']""",
            {"data":data})
```
```

Once complete, you will see new 'Flower_Record' nodes in Neo4j. Each Flower Record contains the various data elements from the original row of data as properties on the new node:

Figure 3.19: *Illustration of Flower Records in Neo4j*

With data stored in this format, we can now expand each of these node properties into new nodes by using Cypher. In this next step, we transform the data from static, row-by-row data into interconnected graph data, which will supercharge our data analytics and machine learning capabilities:

```
```

```
// First, ensure there is a Petal_Length node
MERGE (p:Petal_Length)
ON CREATE SET p.name = 'Petal Length' // You could set properties here
if needed


// Match all Flower_Record nodes and connect them to the Petal_Length
node
WITH p
MATCH (s:Flower_Record)
MERGE (s)-[r:PETAL_LENGTH]->(p)
SET r.Petal_Length = toFloat(s.Petal_Length)
```
```
```

By going through each of these steps, you will create a dense network containing all the Iris dataset records along with the connections to the flower attributes. In a later chapter of this book, we will implement graph algorithms to explore this data further:

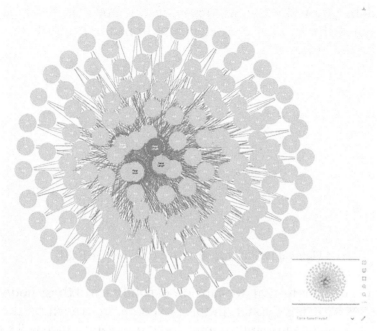

Figure 3.20: *Illustration of the connected Flower elements from the Iris dataset*

Conclusion

Throughout this chapter, we explored data import methodologies, including the Aura DB import tool, Admin Import tool, Pandas Dataframe import, and CSV flat file imports. The Admin Import tool is well-suited for high-performance data ingestion because it eliminates the need for logging. However, the Admin import tool is slightly more complex than other import methods and requires Admin privileges to run the import command. Therefore, it may be worth exploring the best option that works for you and your organization's use case.

Importing data through CSVs and/or Pandas dataframes is a more flexible approach. While this approach is slower due to transaction logging, it is versatile and does not require any administrative privileges. Furthermore, through the import process, data can be conveniently manipulated using Pandas or Cypher to loop through lists or parse specific properties to accommodate your data design.

In the next chapter, we will dive deeper into the Cypher query language for data transformation and retrieval. This is a pivotal step in our analysis, which leverages the true power and speed of graph databases to provide users the requested data at lightning speed.

Points to Remember

- **Graph vs. Relational Databases**: Graph databases such as Neo4j are inherently different from traditional databases. They excel in handling complex relationships and interconnected data. Traditional databases, on the other hand, are optimized for tabular data structures.

- **Features of Neo4j**: Neo4j stands out with its robust set of out-of-the-box features such as ACID compliance, flexible schema, and strong support for relationship traversal.

- **Graph Database Terminology**: Familiarity with terms such as nodes, relationships, properties, and labels is essential for working with graph databases like Neo4j and will serve the reader well for the remainder of this book.

- **Cypher Query Language**: Neo4j utilizes its own query language, Cypher, for efficient traversal of the database. Cypher is crucial for efficient querying, manipulation, and relationship matching in Neo4j.

- **Data Import Process**: Importing data into Neo4j is a non-trivial yet important step in the data analysis process. Understanding best practices and which options work best for a given situation will ensure optimal import performance and faster data insights.

## CHAPTER 4

Cypher Query Language

Introduction

In this chapter, we will discuss the Cypher query language. Cypher is a declarative graph query language that allows for efficient querying and updating of graph databases. It was developed by Neo4j and is used to query the Neo4j database.

Cypher is open and freely available for use. Neo4j has made efforts to make Cypher a standard for querying graph databases by contributing it to an open-source project called openCypher. The openCypher project aims to make the Cypher query language available to a wider community.

Here is an example of a simple Cypher query:

```
MATCH (a:Person)-[r:LIKES]->(b:Person)
WHERE a.name = 'Carl'
RETURN b.name
```

In this query, we return data about people that 'Carl' likes. We first anchor on our person node where the person's name is 'Carl', then expand to other people based on the 'LIKES' relationship and return those people's names.

Structure

In this chapter, we will cover the following topics:

- Basics of cypher path finding queries (MATCH, WHERE, RETURN)
- Advanced cypher path finding queries (COLLECT, CONTAINS, EXISTS)
- Including the count of relationships (or "degree") for nodes
- Generating GDS projections
- Creating "similar" relationships between nodes sharing common attributes
- Cypher query "explain" plans and canceling long-running queries

Key Elements of a Cypher Query

Let's recap some of the key elements of a Cypher query:

- **Nodes**: these are the entities of the graph and are denoted in Cypher using enclosed parentheses with semicolons followed by Node label name, for example, (`:Person`). They hold properties in the form of key-value pairs.

- **Relationships**: Relationships connect nodes explicitly and can contain properties just like Nodes. In Cypher, these are depicted with square brackets and dashes along with greater than (`>`) or less than (`<`) sign to denote the direction, for example, (`p1:Person`)-[`r:CONNECTED_TO`]->(`p2:Person`).

- `MATCH` **clause**: This is somewhat similar to the 'SELECT' statement in SQL. This clause matches the pattern of nodes and relationships you are searching for.

- `RETURN` **Clause**: Specifies the data returned from the query. The MATCH clause identifies the pattern to match on, but the RETURN clause specifies which elements of the pattern should be returned.

- `WHERE` **clause**: This is used in a query to filter the data based on certain criteria or criteria. This is similar to filtering data with SQL. Once the MATCH clause defines a pattern to search for, the WHERE clause limits the results of the search by filtering for only patterns with specific attributes. **NOTE**: It is best practice to set an index on any node or relationship properties used in the WHERE clause to improve query performance.

- `LIMIT` **clause**: This clause will limit the number of responses to ensure the transaction does not bog down the server. This is akin to other limit functions in other languages such as `head()`, TOP 100, and so on.

Getting Started with Cypher

In this section, we will begin writing Cypher queries based on the data loaded in the previous chapter. While Cypher is intuitive to read and follow along with, we recommend that you copy and paste the Cypher queries into your own Neo4j Browser to follow along with this section. Reading the Cypher code and visualizing the results of the query will go a long way in helping you become fluent with Cypher.

Querying Data of Individuals with Cypher

In this section, we will walk through queries step-by-step. First, let's MATCH on the pattern of 'Individual' based on the data loaded in the previous chapter. The query to create this data can also be found in the Jupyter Notebook associated with this chapter.

Once we MATCH on the **'Individual'** label and assign all of these nodes to the variable '**n1**', let's next filter these results to only return nodes where the name equals 'Mitch.' Once complete, we return '*****' or all patterns matched. We also limit the results to 25 just in case there are many nodes matching this criteria. In this case, only one node matches this pattern and is returned as shown in the following figure:

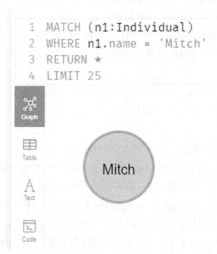

```
1  MATCH (n1:Individual)
2  WHERE n1.name = 'Mitch'
3  RETURN *
4  LIMIT 25
```

Figure 4.1: *Return a single node based on the WHERE clause*

Next, we can again match on the label 'Individual' and return a count of all the individuals in the database as well as a comma-separated list of all the names of the Individuals. First, we match an Individual then use the Cypher functions count() and collect() to aggregate the results of the pattern.

As you can see, we can count the number of nodes in the variable 'n' by using count(n). To collect the 'name' property on each of these nodes, we must specify which property on the 'n' node we would like to collect. In this case, we collect the 'n.name' property.

```
1  MATCH (n:Individual)
2  RETURN count(n) as Number_of_Individuals, collect(n.name) as Names
```

Number_of_Individuals	Names
11	['Mitch', 'Carl', 'Nathan', 'Sophia', 'Emma', 'Olivia', 'James', 'Michael', 'Emily', 'Madison', 'David']

Figure 4.2: *Return a collection of all individuals matching this pattern*

As a simple illustration of this network of individuals, let's return all the 'FRIEND_OF' relationships between these nodes. First, we match the pattern we are interested in. In this case, we assign a variable 'r' to the FRIEND_OF relationship and use '*' to return everything from the match clause. Notice that we did not use the directional arrow in the relationship clause in this example. While you can use the directional arrow, the direction of the 'FRIEND_OF' is not important to the "MATCH' clause. Neo4j requires a direction to be stored under the hood, but it does not need to be specified in the Cypher query:

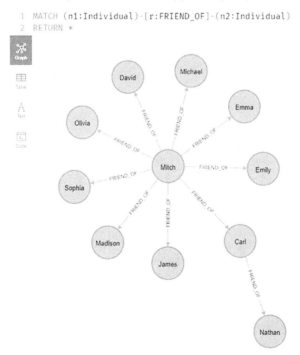

```
1  MATCH (n1:Individual)-[r:FRIEND_OF]-(n2:Individual)
2  RETURN *
```

Figure 4.3: *Network of individuals*

Finally, a data table can be generated from the `MATCH` pattern. In the following example, we can see the direction component was added to the '`FRIEND_OF`' relationship which prevents the pattern from being duplicated in the Cypher response. Furthermore, we use the Cypher function `type()` to specify the type of relationship which can be very helpful in situations where many types of relationships could be used to connect the nodes, for example, `REFERRED_BY, NEIGHBOR_OF, SENT_MESSAGE_TO`:

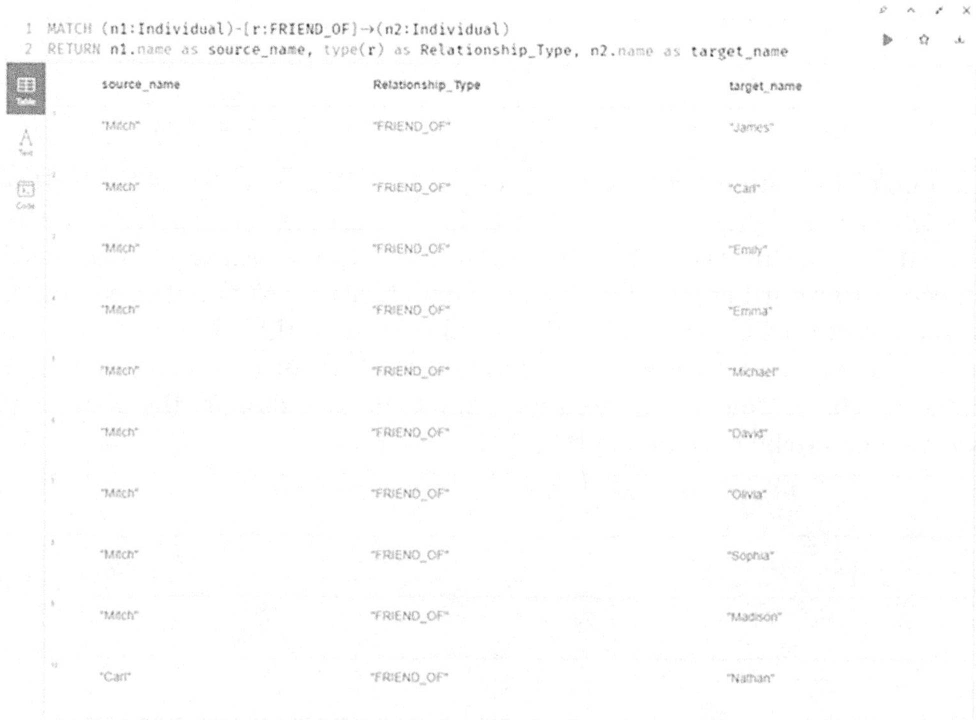

```
MATCH (n1:Individual)-[r:FRIEND_OF]->(n2:Individual)
RETURN n1.name as source_name, type(r) as Relationship_Type, n2.name as target_name
```

source_name	Relationship_Type	target_name
"Mitch"	"FRIEND_OF"	"James"
"Mitch"	"FRIEND_OF"	"Carl"
"Mitch"	"FRIEND_OF"	"Emily"
"Mitch"	"FRIEND_OF"	"Emma"
"Mitch"	"FRIEND_OF"	"Michael"
"Mitch"	"FRIEND_OF"	"David"
"Mitch"	"FRIEND_OF"	"Olivia"
"Mitch"	"FRIEND_OF"	"Sophia"
"Mitch"	"FRIEND_OF"	"Madison"
"Carl"	"FRIEND_OF"	"Nathan"

Figure 4.4: *Illustration of data table using Neo4j Cypher*

Querying Data of Recipes with Cypher

To begin querying Recipe data, we must first ensure that we are connected to the '`recipe`' database rather than the 'neo4j' database. In the following figure, you can select the 'recipe' database manually using the user interface. Alternatively, you can use Cypher to specify the name of the database using the ``` `:use recipe` ``` command:

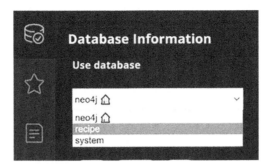

Figure 4.5: *Connect to the 'recipe' database*

Let's take a look at all the recipes for cornbread. I am from the Southeast region of the United States and cornbread has been a staple of my diet for many years. Unlike breads made from wheat flour, cornbread is primarily made from cornmeal which is a flour ground from dried corn/maize. Cornbread is often served as a side dish with meals such as fried chicken, chili, or Thanksgiving turkey. Cornbread is golden brown and crumbly to the touch. It can taste either sweet or savory – but I prefer it sweet like cake.

First, before we search this string for cornbread recipes, we need to set an index on the property 'Recipe_Title.' Indexing is a critical feature for enhancing the performance of data retrieval queries. Without an index, the query might have to scan every node in the database to search for the requested property, which becomes increasingly impractical as the size of the data grows.

```
```CREATE INDEX Recipe_Title IF NOT EXISTS FOR (n:Recipe) ON
(n.Recipe_Title) ```
```

Next, ensure that the index has populated fully before running any queries that require this index. Use the ```SHOW INDEX``` command to ensure that the index has been populated fully:

Figure 4.6: *Show index*

Once the index shows the state "ONLINE", then run the following query to identify 100 of the recipes that contain the word 'cornbread' in the recipe title:
```

Figure 4.7: *Cornbread Recipes - Limit to 100*

We can now check to see exactly how many recipes contain cornbread in the title:

Figure 4.8: *Return count of recipes containing cornbread in the title*

There are 8,688 recipes to make cornbread in this database. It looks like I am not the only person who enjoys cornbread! Let's next look at the directions and ingredients for one of these recipes:

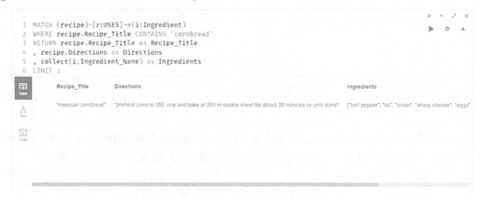

Figure 4.9: *Show the directions and ingredients for one of the cornbread recipes*

As we can see, this recipe calls for "sharp cheese" as one of the ingredients. Also, the directions are a bit limited for this recipe. Let's rewrite this query to request a recipe with at least 500 characters (more directions) as well as a different type of cheese (not "sharp cheese"):

```
gds.set_database('recipe')

gds.run_cypher("""
MATCH (recipe)-[r:USES]->(i:Ingredient)
WHERE recipe.Recipe_Title CONTAINS 'cornbread'
    AND size(recipe.Directions) > 500
    AND i.Ingredient_Name <> 'sharp cheese'
RETURN recipe.Recipe_Title as Recipe_Title
, recipe.Directions as Directions
, collect(i.Ingredient_Name) as Ingredients
ORDER BY Recipe_Title
LIMIT 3
""")
```

	Recipe_Title	Directions	Ingredients
0	"first" skillet cornbread	heat oven to 400 degrees f, in 8 cast iron skillet over medium heat, cook bacon until crisp transfer to paper towles to drain crumble, remove all but 1 12 teaspoons bacon drippings, brush sides and bottom of pan with remaining drippings, place skillet in over for 5 minutes, meanwhile, in medium bowl, stir together cornbread mix, mexicorn, jalapeno, egg, cheese, milk, and bacon until combined, spoon batter into heated skillet and bake 15 minutes, or until golden, trade the jalapenos and cheese for fillings that taste best with your summer feast, garlic lover stir 2oz shredded provolone cheese, 1tsp italian seasoning, and 1 clove minced garlic into batter until just combined, like it hot stir 2 oz diced or shredded pepper jack cheese, 12 teaspoons southwest chipotle seasoning like mrs dash, and 1 tsp whole mexican oregano,like mccormick, into batter until just combined, subtle more your style stir 2oz shredded gruyere cheese, 1tsp herbes de provence and 12 teaspoons seasoned pepper blend into batter until just combined	[egg, milk, corn, bacon, cheddar cheese, jalapeno pepper]
1	"hot" mexican cornbread	preheat oven to 400, brown and drain ground chuck, then add the salt and pepper seasoning along with chopped onion, cook slowly until ground beef and onion have cooked through, pour crisco in a 13 x 9inch cake pan and heat, when crisco is hot, pour about half into cornbread batter and mix, then pour about 12 of batter into pan, add your ground chuck and seasonings, then add your drained mexican corn, slice velveeta cheese to cover mixture, then add remaining cornbread batter, cook until golden brown allow to cool cut into squares	[batch, Velveeta cheese, salt, ground chuck, liquid, onion, corn]
2	"jiffy" roasted corn and jalapeno cornbread	melt butter in a saute pan, add the corn, onion and red pepper and saute on medium heat until some of the corn kernels start to turn golden brown, whisk egg, corn liquid, and cream together, stir into corn muffin mix with a fork, stir in diced jalapenos and cheddar cheese, quickly stir in hot sauteed corn and onion mixture, just mixing in slightly, pour into 8 x 8 buttered baking dish, bake at 350 for 15 minutes, remove cornbread, turn off oven, drizzle cornbread with honey and put back in hot oven for 5 minutes if you prefer not to use honey just bake for a total of 20 minutes, remove from oven and let stand for 10 minutes before serving, note you may want to use 112 cups frozen corn in place of the canned corn just use 14 cup milk in place of the 14 cup reserved corn liquid	[honey, heavy cream, red bell pepper, butter, egg, whole kernel corn, corn muffin, jalapenos, onion, cheddar cheese]

Figure 4.10: *Return cornbread recipes*

In this illustration, we see three cornbread recipes sorted in alphabetical order by using the ORDER BY clause. We can also see the Directions are longer in these results because we specified the size() must be more than 500 characters. Lastly, we use the ```gds.set_database()``` command to specify the query run against the 'recipe' database.

Many of these recipes are quite similar. In the next section, we will dive into a technique to quantify the similarity between recipes.

Advanced Querying and Data Manipulation with Cypher

Congratulations on completing the beginning steps of your Cypher journey! The information we covered so far will provide the foundational building blocks for the topics we cover moving forward. At its heart, graph data science is the study of graph traversals and understanding the implications of the relationship between nodes. Now that you know the basics of writing patterns in Cypher and returning the attributes, you can understand the further nuances in the Cypher query language will allow you to implement more powerful techniques and algorithms.

Advanced Filtering

As with traditional relational databases, Neo4j offers many filtering options. The WHERE clause operates much like its SQL counterpart, used to filter data based on specific conditions where the conditions are met. You can set conditions using the operators such as:

- =
- >
- <
- <>
- >=
- <=
- LIKE
- CONTAINS
- EXISTS

The **AND**, **OR**, and **NOT** logical operators can be used within the **WHERE** clause to combine or exclude conditions and provide more flexibility to your query. For example, you might have a situation where you need to match on combinations of criteria:

```
` ` `
MATCH (n:Recipe)
WHERE n.Recipe_Title = 'broccoli casserole'
    AND (n.Recipe_ID < 10000
    OR n.Source = 'gathered')
RETURN n
LIMIT 25
` ` `
```

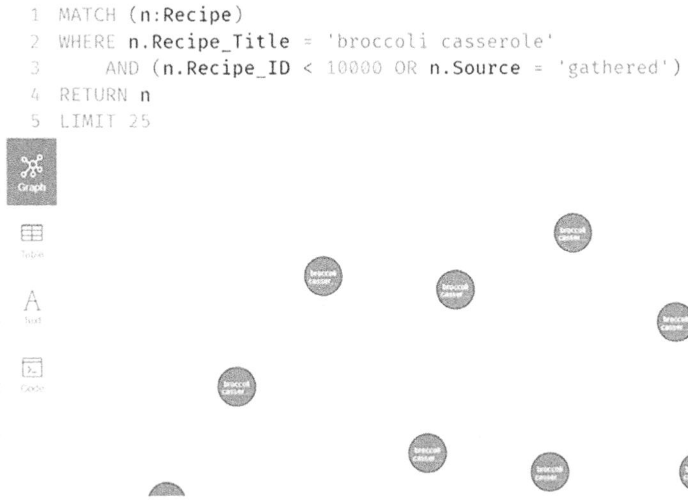

Figure 4.11: *Example of filtering based on multiple criteria*

Furthermore, you may have a situation where you need to match some criteria and exclude other criteria:

```
` ` `
MATCH (n:Recipe)
WHERE n.Recipe_Title = 'broccoli casserole'
    AND not n.Source = 'gathered'
RETURN n
LIMIT 25
` ` `
```

In this query, we anchor on the Recipe nodes where the title of the recipe is 'broccoli casserole' but the source of the recipe does not equal 'gathered.' We then return the first 25 nodes that match this criteria:

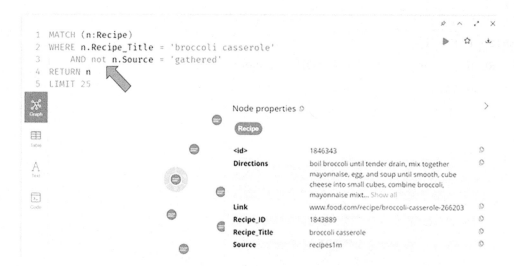

```
1  MATCH (n:Recipe)
2  WHERE n.Recipe_Title = 'broccoli casserole'
3      AND not n.Source = 'gathered'
4  RETURN n
5  LIMIT 25
```

Figure 4.12: *Example of the 'NOT' exclusion criteria*

You may encounter situations where you need to filter for results based on partial lists or multiple matches. In this section, we will use the recipe database to filter for recipes that contain a list of ingredients.

Let's find a recipe that contains both almonds and walnuts. With a package of each in the pantry and both being is unsalted, the aim is to find a recipe that combines these two ingredients into a roasted mix.

In this query, we first match our recipes with our ingredients in a pattern match. Next, we filter for only ingredient nodes that are almonds or walnuts and where the recipe title contains the word 'spice.' Once the initial pattern is returned, we use the WITH keyword to gather the results of this query and collect all of the ingredients into a list called 'ingredients.' Finally, we use the ALL() function to ensure the target ingredients are each contained in the collected list of ingredients. As a reminder, RETURN() is required at the end of the query to determine which elements of the matched set should be returned. In this case, we return a dataset and limit the results to the first 10 records.

```
```

```
MATCH (recipe:Recipe)-[:USES]->(i:Ingredient)
WHERE i.Ingredient_Name IN ['almonds', 'walnuts']
    AND recipe.Recipe_Title CONTAINS 'spice'
WITH recipe, collect(i.Ingredient_Name) as ingredients
```

```
WHERE ALL(ingredient IN ['almonds', 'walnuts'] WHERE ingredient IN
ingredients)
RETURN recipe.Recipe_Title as Recipe_Title, recipe.Directions as Direc-
tions, recipe.Link as Link
LIMIT 10
```

Recipe_Title	Directions
"fall harvest spice cake"	"preheat oven to 375 degrees, grease and flour two 9 inch round baking pans"
"honey roasted spiced nuts recipe"	"preheat oven to 325f, line a baking sheet with parchment paper, combine all ingredients in a medium"
"lebanon's new mama spiced tea (ainar)"	"add spices to water use a tea ball if you have one and bring to a boil, cover and simmer 15 minutes"
"no guilt spiced mixed nuts"	"preheat oven to 225 degrees f 110 degrees c line a baking sheet with waxed paper, mix brown sugar"
"spiced nuts"	"preheat oven to 300, combine egg white and water, mix nuts and toss in egg white to coat, mix sugar"

Figure 4.13: *Results of the spiced nuts query*

The 'honey roasted spiced nuts recipe' sounds delicious. Let's take a look at all of the ingredients involved:

```
MATCH (n:Recipe) WHERE n.Recipe_Title = "honey roasted spiced nuts
recipe" RETURN n
```

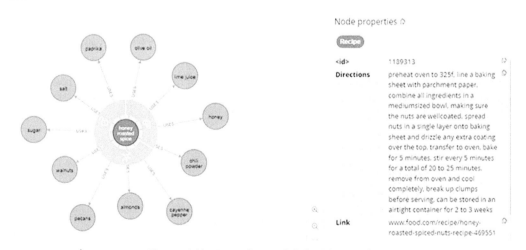

Figure 4.14: *Honey Roasted Spice Nuts recipe*

Degree Functions

Degree functions are a way to capture the number of incoming and outgoing relationships to a node. The following recipe illustration, for example, has an outgoing degree of 6. As you can see, 6 relationships are leaving the source node and going to the target nodes. Degree functions can be divided into three categories:

- **Outgoing Degree**: This is the total number of relationships leaving the source node

- **Incoming Degree**: This is the total number of relationships going toward the source node (in the following example, zero)

- **Degree**: The total number of incoming AND outgoing relationships

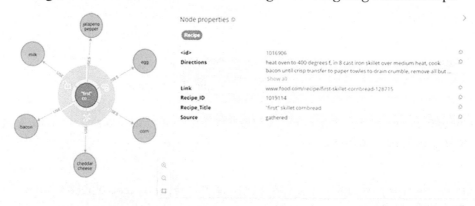

Figure 4.15: *Illustration of a node with out_degree = 6*

Next, let's write Cypher code to determine the degree of each recipe in our 'recipe' database. To accomplish this, we will use the SIZE() function to represent the number of patterns that were included in the matched pattern. We will limit the command to only nodes containing the word 'cornbread' in the Recipe_Title to reduce the query response time:

```
```

MATCH (recipe)-[r:USES]->(i:Ingredient)

WHERE recipe.Recipe_Title CONTAINS 'cornbread'

WITH recipe, apoc.node.degree(recipe) as degree

SET recipe.degree = degree

```
```

We now have the degree of the node for each cornbread recipe. In the following image, we can see the recipe with the highest degree and number of ingredients:

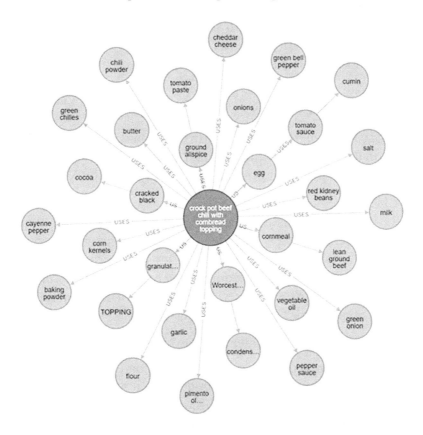

Figure 4.16: *The recipe with the highest number of ingredients*

To discover this recipe, we can use the cypher query as follows:

```
MATCH (r:Recipe)
WHERE r.degree is not null
WITH max(r.degree) as max_degree

MATCH (r:Recipe)-[u:USES]->(i:Ingredient)
WHERE r.degree = max_degree
RETURN r,u,i
```

In this query, we first match the recipes which contain the degree property. Next, we discover which node has the highest degree by using the `max()` function. Once we know the max degree, we then match it to the recipe where the degree matches the max degree and expand to all the connected ingredients. Finally, we return the recipe (variable r), ingredients (variable i), as well as the relationships between the two nodes (variable u).

Graph Projections

Graph projections in Neo4j represent the stored graph data in a format optimized for the execution of graph algorithms. Similar to creating a "**view**" in a relational database, the graph projection is created and managed by the Neo4j **Graph Data Science (GDS)** library.

While a native graph model is efficient for graph traversals and analysis, this method of storage is not always the most efficient for executing many graph algorithms. For example, many graph algorithms require knowledge of the degree of each node (recall this is the number of relationships connected to the node). The graph projections are stored in a more algorithm-friendly format in memory, such as an adjacency matrix.

Neo4j offers two types of graph projection methods:

- **Native graph projections**: These use the existing graph structure and labels and are the most computationally efficient method of projection.
- **Cypher projections**: These offer the user flexibility to define the specific pattern of nodes and relationships to push to memory.

First, let's take a look at the Native Projection method using the recipe database schema to illustrate. As you can see, we need to set the name of the projection, followed by the node types/labels, followed by the relationships to include in our analysis:

```
```

CALL gds.graph.project(
    'recipeGraph', // The name of the graph projection.
    ['Recipe', 'Ingredient'], // The node labels to include.
    {USES: {orientation: 'UNDIRECTED'}} // The relationship types to
include.
);
```
```

When we run this graph projection, we can see 2.3 million nodes and 21 million relationships were passed into graph data science memory:

nodeProjection	relationshipProjection	graphName	nodeCount	relationshipCount	projectMillis
{	{	"recipeGraph"	2366780	20914926	7457

```
{                          {
  "Recipe": {                "USES": {
    "label":                   "orientation":
  "Recipe",                  "UNDIRECTED",
    "properties":              "indexInverse":
  {                          false,
                               "aggregation":
    }                        "DEFAULT",
  },                           "type": "USES",
  "Ingredient": {              "properties": {
    "label":
  "Ingredient",                }
    "properties":            }
  {                        }

    }
  }
}
```

Figure 4.17: *The output of the graph projection command*

Next, let's look at the Cypher Projection method. Again, the first line sets the name of the projection. The second line specifies the nodes to use in the projection using Cypher. The third line represents the full pattern to use the projection using Cypher.

As you can see, this method is highly flexible as you can write a Cypher query to match the specific pattern you are looking to analyze. However, there are limitations to this approach, including the inability to specify 'UNDIRECTED', which is important for some graph algorithms, as we will see in later chapters. Additionally, this approach is not as computationally efficient as the native projection method and, therefore, may prove infeasible for your analysis based on the size/scale of your database:

```
```
MATCH (r1:Recipe)-[:USES]->(i:Ingredient)<-[:USES]-(r2:Recipe)
WITH gds.graph.project('projectedGraph', r1, r2) AS g
WHERE r1.degree is not null
  AND r2.degree is not null
```
```

```
RETURN
  g.graphName AS graph, g.nodeCount AS nodes, g.relationshipCount AS
rels
```

With this flexible approach, we can now limit the graph projection to only the recipes which contain the degree property. As the following image illustrates, this reduces the size of the graph projection dramatically to only 6208 nodes:

graph	nodes	rels
"projectedGraph"	6208	27283918

Figure 4.18: The output of the graph projection command

The Cypher projection method can be a helpful tool in situations where you only need to push a subset of the graph into memory. It adds flexibility to the graph data science pipeline.

Creating SIMILAR_RECIPE Relationship

In this section, we will compare the ingredients of the various recipes and create a new relationship between similar recipes. For each recipe, we will be able to quantify the number of similar ingredients.

First, we need to create a graph projection so that we can use the Jaccard Similarity algorithm to find similar recipes. This algorithm calculates the similarity between nodes based on the intersection of shared attributes. In the case of the recipe data, the similarity of recipes would be calculated based on the count of shared ingredients. We will use the Cypher Projection method in this example as a means to limit the amount of data pushed to memory for this example.

In the following query, we create a graph projection named 'cornbreadGraph' to only project recipes that contain the word 'cornbread' in the recipe title. Recall that we set the degree of the recipes that contain the word 'cornbread' and set an index on the property 'degree.' We will use this property to limit the number of nodes returned in the graph projection. Furthermore, we will limit to only recipes with a degree of greater than 10 to further reduce the computational complexity for this illustration.

Remember, it is very important to index properties used in the WHERE clause of your queries. **If you forget to index these properties, then the Neo4j database could crash** because the database needs to search through each node label for the property listed:

```
```

CALL gds.graph.project.cypher(
    'cornbreadGraph',
    'MATCH (r:Recipe) WHERE r.degree > 10 RETURN id(r) AS id',
    'MATCH (r1:Recipe)-[:USES]->(i:Ingredient)<-[:USES]-(r2:Recipe)
    WHERE r1.degree > 10 AND r2.degree > 10
    RETURN id(r1) AS source, id(r2) AS target'
);
```
```

```
gds.run_cypher("""
CALL gds.graph.project.cypher(
    'cornbreadGraph',
    'MATCH (r:Recipe) WHERE r.degree > 10 RETURN id(r) AS id',
    'MATCH (r1:Recipe)-[:USES]->(i:Ingredient)<-[:USES]-(r2:Recipe)
    WHERE r1.degree > 10 AND r2.degree > 10
    RETURN id(r1) AS source, id(r2) AS target'
);
""")
```

	nodeQuery	relationshipQuery	graphName	nodeCount	relationshipCount
0	MATCH (r:Recipe) WHERE r.degree > 10 RETURN id(r) AS id	MATCH (r1:Recipe)-[:USES]->(i:Ingredient) <-[:USES]-(r2:Recipe) \n WHERE r1.degree > 10 AND r2.degree > 10 \n RETURN id(r1) AS source, id(r2) AS target	cornbreadGraph	1230	3933770

Figure 4.19: *Cypher Projection for Cornbread Recipe Similarity*

In this projection, there were 1230 recipe nodes and 3,933,770 relationships to other recipe nodes. The large number of relationships is due to the large number of shared ingredients. It is helpful to count the number of nodes prior to writing projections to ensure the projection is not much larger than expected. In this case, this can be accomplished with the following query:

```
` ` `
MATCH (r1:Recipe)-[:USES]->(i:Ingredient)<-[:USES]-(r2:Recipe)
WHERE r1.degree > 10
    AND r2.degree > 10
    AND id(r1) < id(r2)
RETURN count(distinct r1) as Recipe_Count
` ` `
```

This query returns the response:

Recipe_Count

1228

Figure 4.20: *Query response for the total number of recipes meeting the criteria*

Now that we have a graph projection of all the recipes containing the word 'cornbread' with more than 10 ingredients, let's run the Jaccard Similarity algorithm to discover very similar recipes based on their shared ingredients. In short, the algorithm calculates the overlap/pair-wise similarities between the two nodes that share common connections. To learn more about the algorithm, you can refer to the Neo4j documentation at: https://neo4j.com/docs/graph-data-science/current/algorithms/node-similarity/.

The following code leverages the 'cornbreadGraph' projection we created. We have set a parameter, similarityCutoff, to 90%. This means that the SIMILAR_TO relationship will only be created by connecting a recipe to another recipe if and only if the number of shared ingredients between the source recipe is greater than or equal to 90% of the same ingredients as the target recipe. If the recipes share greater than or equal to 90% of the same ingredients, then a new relationship is created between the recipes and the property 'similarity' is set on the relationship to specify the match percentage:

```
` ` `
CALL gds.nodeSimilarity.write('cornbreadGraph', {
    writeRelationshipType: 'SIMILAR_TO',
    writeProperty: 'similarity',
    similarityCutoff: 0.90
```

```
})
YIELD nodesCompared, relationshipsWritten;
```
` ` `

Once the SIMILAR_TO relationship has been created, we can query a handful of these recipes. This will not return all the recipes that are similar or within the same community/cluster but will be helpful for us to visually inspect. We can run this query to take a closer look at the results:

` ` `

```
MATCH p=()-[r:SIMILAR_TO]->() RETURN p LIMIT 25
```
` ` `

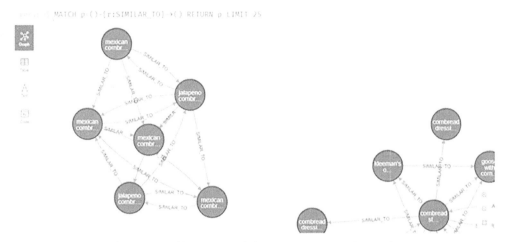

Figure 4.21: *Illustration of the SIMILAR_TO relationship*

It appears that we have a small cluster/community of similar cornbread recipes titled 'mexican cornbread' and 'jalapeno cornbread.' As you can see, Neo4j's ability to algorithmically identify similarities can save you an enormous amount of time and energy by consolidating similar records in your database. In a later chapter, we will explore the topic of 'Entity Resolution', which similarly takes a set of similar nodes and seeks to consolidate into a single master entity.

Let's take a closer look at the ingredients in these similar recipes. This can be accomplished in Neo4j Browser by selecting the recipe node and then clicking the 'expand' option in the tooltip:

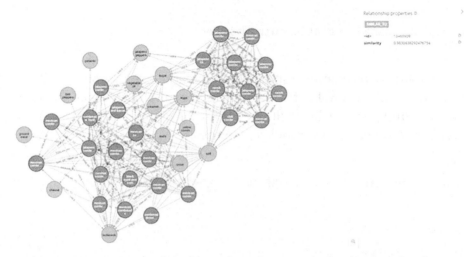

Figure 4.22: *Examine the shared ingredients between similar Cornbread recipes*

It appears that many of these jalapeno/mexican cornbread recipes use a combination of the following ingredients:

- Jalapeno Peppers
- Yellow Cornmeal
- Eggs
- Creamstyle
- Soda
- Onion
- Vegetable Oil
- Sugar

As you can see, some recipes use pimento, bell peppers, or ground meat, but not all recipes. This is why we see similarity measures ranging from 90% to 100%. Not all the recipes use the same ingredients, but it makes sense that similar recipes would leverage similar ingredients.

Canceling Long-Running Queries

While Neo4j is extremely efficient, you may encounter long-running queries and need to cancel the queries. You can view the queries that are currently running by using ```show transactions``` or ```:queries``` in the Neo4j Browser or Cypher Shell. This returns all active queries, start times, the CPU used, and other helpful information:

Figure 4.23: *Show actively running queries*

To kill or cancel a long-running query, you can use the ```dbms.killQuery(queryId)``` command and insert the `queryId` discovered from the ```CALL dbms.listQueries()``` command.

Canceling a query in Neo4j is a cooperative operation where the query checks in intervals whether it should halt. Some operations, however, might be unresponsive to termination requests for quite some time. Therefore, it's a good idea to monitor query performance, optimize queries before executing them, and manage database resources to minimize the necessity of query cancellations.

If you have tried canceling the query to no avail, then you can also restart the database. Restarting the database clears transient states, resets connections, and allows new configurations to take effect, which will effectively resolve the long-running query issue. If you are running Neo4j on a server and have administrator privileges, then you can use the ```neo4j restart``` command. If you are running Neo4j from the browser, then you can click this restart button:

Figure 4.24: *Restart database*

Explaining Queries Before Executing

It is good practice to explain queries before executing them in any database management system, including Neo4j. This allows you to gain insight into the operations of the database server plan before running the query. This enables you to optimize the performance of the queries as well as predict the impact on the database system.

In Neo4j, you can add 'EXPLAIN' before the Cypher query to obtain a detailed breakdown of the database's execution plan without the overhead of actually executing the query. This will provide an execution strategy that tells you the plan to retrieve the data, including the nodes, relationships, and properties the query will touch:

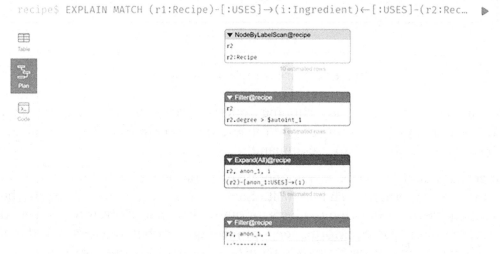

Figure 4.25: *Illustration of the 'EXPLAIN' cypher query functionality*

Similarly, the 'PROFILE' command also provides an execution plan. However, 'PROFILE' goes one step further and executes the query and provides statistics on the database at each stage:

```
1  PROFILE MATCH (r1:Recipe)-[:USES]→(i:Ingredient)←[:USES]-(r2:Recipe)
2        WHERE r1.degree > 10
3            AND r2.degree > 10
4            AND id(r1) < id(r2)
5  RETURN *
6  LIMIT 100
```

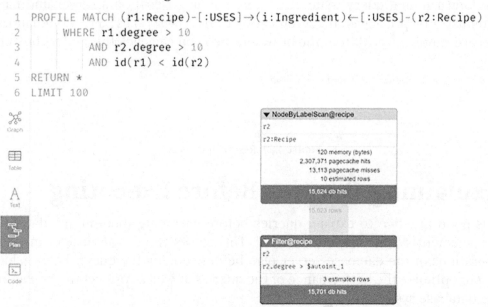

Figure 4.26: *Illustration of the 'PROFILE' cypher query functionality*

In a graph database like Neo4j, explaining and profiling queries are critical operations due to the potential for exponential growth when traversing relationships. Understanding the path of the query and the number of hits on the database will help you avoid inadvertently executing a query that could consume significant resources and potentially require a reboot of the database.

Conclusion

This chapter serves as an in-depth guide to mastering Cypher, which is the query language for Neo4j graph databases. The chapter introduces the essential components of a Cypher query such as nodes, relationships, properties, and key clauses such as `MATCH`, `RETURN`, `WHERE`, and `LIMIT`.

The chapter provides many practical tips and applications. The chapter advises leveraging properties to speed up query performance and uses the recipe dataset to illustrate how to practically implement these solutions. Advanced techniques, such as using the degree function to understand the number of relationships connected to a node, are covered. Additionally, graph projections and their significance are covered as a way to execute graph algorithms efficiently. Both native and cypher projections are introduced as well as the advantages and disadvantages of each.

The chapter also explores creating relationships between similar recipes in the Recipe dataset based on the Jaccard Similarity algorithm, emphasizing the power of graph databases in identifying patterns and similarities that would otherwise be extremely difficult to uncover in traditional relational databases.

Whether you're a beginner, just getting started with Cypher or looking to deepen your understanding of Neo4j, this chapter provides the foundational knowledge and practical skills needed to become proficient in querying and manipulating graph databases.

In the next chapter, we will dive into graph visualization, which plays a crucial role in communicating the data structures and insights to stakeholders, as well as assisting with exploratory analysis.

Points to Remember

- **Cypher Queries**: Cypher is a powerful query language for Neo4j, and understanding the basic components of the path finding queries, such as `MATCH`, `RETURN`, `WHERE`, and `LIMIT`, are foundational to querying the graph database.

- **Leverage Properties of Nodes and Relationships**: Optimizing query performance is critical to the success of graph database projects. If you index your database properties correctly, then you will be able to run your queries orders of magnitude more quickly than if you do not include indexes. Both nodes and relationships can store properties which can then be indexed.

- **Understanding GDS Projections**: Both GDS and Cypher projections are foundational to effective graph analysis. Understanding the differences, advantages, and disadvantages of each approach will enable you to perform effective and efficient graph analysis.

- **Creating "Similar" Relationships**: This chapter explores the creation of similar relationships using the Jaccard Similarity algorithm and highlights the native graph database's ability to unearth patterns that are challenging (and oftentimes impossible) to detect in traditional databases.

- **Query Management**: The Cypher query "explain" plans and the ability to cancel long-running queries will enable you to manage and optimize the performance of your queries.

Visualizing Graph Networks

Introduction

Visualization of data plays a pivotal role in data science. It helps us translate the complicated dimensions of data into understandable, digestible, and actionable insights. In this chapter, we will take a journey into the visualization of complex graph data by combining Python's versatile programming capabilities with Neo4j's graph data modeling.

Whether you're a beginner in the art of data visualization or a seasoned professional, this chapter aims to provide a comprehensive guide to navigating the intricacies of graph data representation. These visualizations will yield meaningful narratives from complex data for a deeper understanding and enhanced decision-making capabilities.

Structure

In this chapter, we will cover the following topics:

- Setting Up Neo4j Bloom
- Saving Cypher Queries in Bloom
- Formatting Bloom Visualizations
- Rules-based Formatting in Bloom
- Exporting CSVs from Bloom
- Power BI Data Import
- Power BI Graph Visualizations

Graph Visualizations with Bloom

One of the most intuitive and effective tools at our disposal in exploring graph visualization is Neo4j Bloom. This is a state-of-the-art graph exploration tool enabling us to visualize and investigate data stored in Neo4j. Neo4j Bloom offers an engaging user interface and enables users to grasp the broader picture. Neo4j is appealing to both technical and non-technical audiences because it enables point-and-click query abilities as well as sophisticated Cypher queries within a visually appealing user interface.

Neo4j Bloom comes free with the Neo4j Desktop version. If your organization requires a Neo4j Server, then you will need a license key to leverage Neo4j Bloom.

In this section, we will walk through the process of opening Bloom, using its features to interact with Neo4j data, and customize the functionality on the Nodes and Relationships to make the visualizations as appealing as possible.

Setting Up Neo4j Bloom

The setup process for Neo4j Bloom, similar to Neo4j Browser, is designed to be user-friendly and uncomplicated. Bloom comes as part of the Neo4j Desktop and Neo4j Aura package, so no additional installation is required. Simply click the **Open** dropdown and select **Neo4j Bloom**:

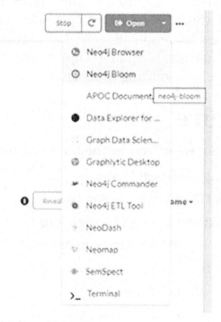

Figure 5.1: *Open Neo4j Bloom*

First, we need to navigate to the correct and corresponding database for analysis. In this section, we will use the recipe database. This requires us to navigate to the Bloom main page to select the recipe database using the following steps:

1. Click the **Settings** button in the top left corner.

2. Click **neo4j** to navigate back to the Bloom home page.

3. Select **recipe** from the list of available databases.

4. Select **Create** and then select '**Blank Perspective**'.

5. Open the newly created perspective:

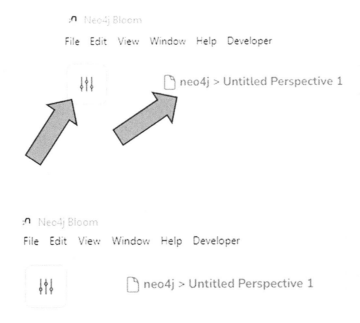

Figure 5.2: Steps 1 and 2: Navigate back to the Bloom Main Page

Select recipe from the dropdown menu. This will switch Bloom to the recipe database instead of pointing to the database named neo4j:

Figure 5.3: Step 3: Select recipe from the list of databases

Click the **Create** button to generate a new and blank perspective:

Figure 5.4: *Step 4: Create a blank perspective*

Next, we will add the Nodes and Relationships we want to include in Bloom. As you can see, Bloom provides the flexibility to exclude nodes, relationships, and properties that we wish to hide from end-users. This feature can be useful when developing new machine learning models and writing their outputs as properties to the nodes in the database. You may not want to confuse or overload users with this new detail, so hiding these properties on the node from users can be beneficial:

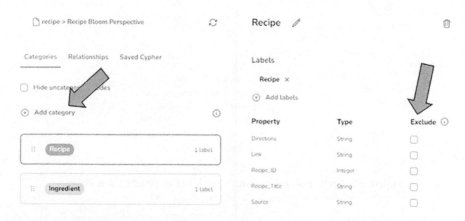

Figure 5.5: *Add categories to Bloom and exclude properties from the nodes*

Saving Cypher Queries in Bloom

Next, we will save a Cypher query to make a network appear on our blank canvas. While Neo4j Browser enables users to quickly match the first 25 nodes associated with a given label through a simple click, Bloom requires an initial Cypher query to initiate the data exploration process. To illustrate this, let us use the following Cypher query related to cornbread:

```
MATCH (recipe)-[r:USES]->(i:Ingredient)
WHERE recipe.Recipe_Title CONTAINS 'cornbread'
    AND size(recipe.Directions) > 500  //only include recipes with
decent, lengthy directions
    AND i.Ingredient_Name <> 'sharp cheese'  //exclude sharp cheese
recipes
RETURN *
LIMIT 1000  //limit the number of results
```

We will now include the Cypher code as a **Saved Cypher** search phrase. This will allow us to render the result of the query on the Bloom canvas:

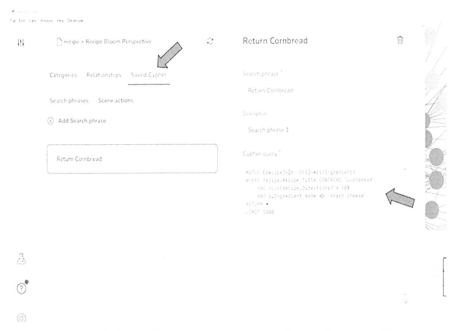

Figure 5.6: *Click Saved Cypher to return a graph visualization in Bloom*

Once you have saved the Cypher query in the **Saved Cypher** panel, return to the blank canvas of Bloom. You will see a search bar at the top left corner of the page. Select the **Return Cornbread** option:

Figure 5.7: *Select the Bloom Saved Query, 'Return Cornbread'*

Once you have selected your Cypher query, click Enter, and you will see the results of the query appear in Bloom.

Formatting Your Bloom Visualization

Once you have the visualization appear on your blank canvas in Bloom, you will notice that the nodes are blank circles. We can alter:

- The icons that appear in these circles
- The size of the circles based on node property values
- The width of the relationship based on the properties of the relationship
- The color of the relationship

First, we can change the icons that appear in the circles by selecting an **Icon** to explain the node label. At the bottom right, click the '**Expand**' button to show the right pane. Next, select the node you would like to style. Finally, click the icon dropdown, type the name of an icon to explain your node label, and select the icon:

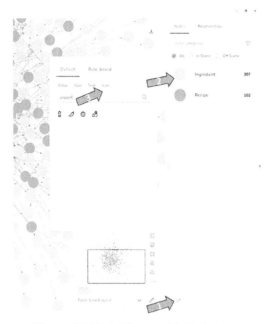

Figure 5.8: *Style Bloom with Node icons*

In addition to labeling the nodes with a helpful Icon, Bloom also allows you to include text on the node. First, select the **Text** dropdown. Next, choose the node property to populate on the node. In the following example, we use the **Ingredient Name** property to appear on the Ingredient nodes:

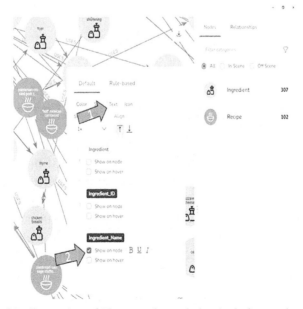

Figure 5.9: *Illustration of Bloom nodes styled to include text descriptions*

We also have the ability to alter the size of the nodes based on the node label. For example, it might be appropriate to reduce the size of the Ingredient nodes rather than the size of the Recipe node in this case, since multiple ingredients are included in each recipe:

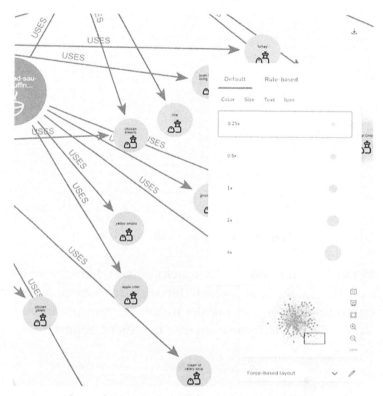

Figure 5.10: *Reduce the size of the nodes in Bloom*

Rules-based Formatting in Bloom

Neo4j Bloom empowers users to represent graph data with rules-based formatting and customize the graph's appearance based on specific criteria or conditions. Discerning specific types of nodes becomes tedious as the graphs grow in size and complexity. In *Figure 5.10*, we can already see how difficult it can be to identify the nodes we are most interested in exploring. By highlighting the distinctions, data patterns, and insights using rules-based formatting, we can direct the users' eyes and attention to the most meaningful aspects of the graph.

If you navigate to the **Rule-based** section, you can select the property on which you would like to set a rule. The rule can then alter the size or color of the node. In *Figure 5.11*, we increase the size of nodes with more than 10 connections ("degree") to four times the original size of the node. This will make the nodes with several ingredients pop off the page:

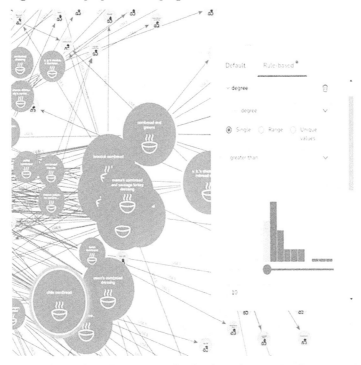

Figure 5.11: *Illustration of rules-based sizing in Bloom*

Similarly, we can add another rule to color the nodes-based on specific conditions. In the following example, we highlight the recipes containing the word `mexican` to help us pinpoint the exact types of recipes we are most interested in experimenting with:

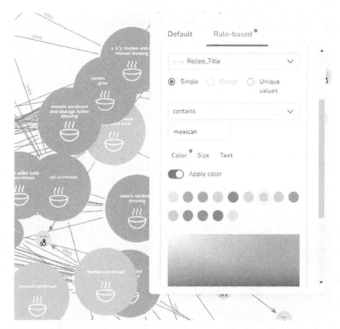

Figure 5.12: *Illustration of string search for color formatting in Bloom. If the title contains the word mexican, then the node is colored green*

Expanding Nodes in Bloom with Expand and Scene Actions

One of the most helpful features of Bloom is the ability to expand nodes to explore the data and incrementally discover new connections in the data. Here are the steps:

1. Hold down the Ctrl key on your keyboard and select a handful of nodes.

2. Reduce the number of nodes on our canvas by right-clicking and selecting **Dismiss Other Nodes**:

Figure 5.13: *Dismiss other nodes in Bloom*

Now that we have only a handful of nodes on our canvas, we can once again select all the nodes, right-click, and navigate to **Expand** → **USES** relationship. This will expand from the recipe nodes to all the ingredients by expanding on the **USES** relationship:

Figure 5.14: *Expand on nodes in Bloom*

As we can see in the following figure, the visualization now shows all of the ingredients involved in each of these recipes. From this manual exploration, we can learn about a few of the ingredients shared among the recipes:

- Onion
- Peppers
- Cheddar cheese
- Salt
- Milk
- Eggs

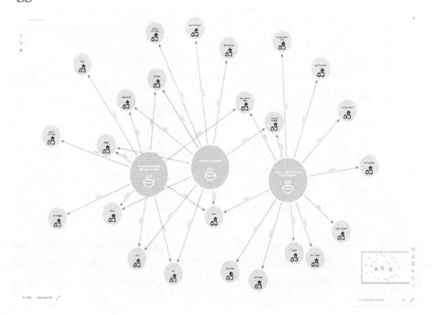

Figure 5.15: *Expanded mexican cornbread recipe nodes*

Scene actions will take this manual exploration one step further. They allow us to use Cypher to control the patterns returned on the canvas. This is extremely powerful and helpful in larger graphs where one node can be connected to hundreds or thousands of other nodes. The scene actions enable us to control the expansion of nodes with precision.

The first step in creating a scene action is to navigate to the **Saved Cypher** dropdown, select **Scene Actions**, and then select **Add Scene Action**:

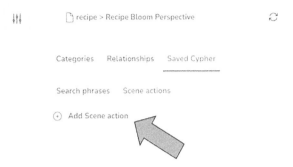

Figure 5.16: *Create a new scene action in Bloom*

Let's write a scene action to expand and return only the shared ingredients between two recipes. This is helpful in situations where we do not want to clutter the visualization by expanding to all of the connected nodes. We only want to return the data where there is shared information between the nodes. Once we add this scene action, we will be able to click to expand to only view the shared ingredients:

Figure 5.17: *Scene action to return common connections between selected nodes*

We can now highlight the two or more recipes where we want to view the common ingredients by holding down the Ctrl key and selecting each node. Next, right-click the node and select our new scene action.

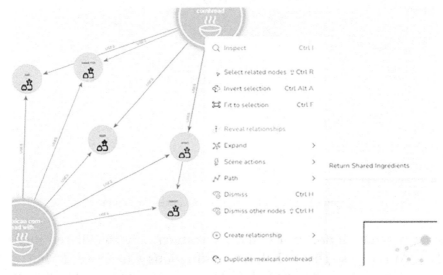

Figure 5.18: *Select the new scene action*

Visualizing with Power BI

Power BI is an exceptional business intelligence (BI) tool featured by Microsoft. While there are certain aspects lacking in Power BI's graph visualization toolkit, the pros of this tool can often outweigh the cons.

Power BI does not support a dynamic API connection to the Neo4j database, which means the data must first be exported to CSV in order to be imported into Power BI. However, many organizations already have Power BI installed in their technology stack, which makes it a straightforward architecture decision – especially during the proof-of-concept phase of development.

To begin, we need to first create a graph dataset. You can either export the results of the **Return Cornbread** command from Bloom, or you can use the Excel file included in the associated chapter reference information for this book:

Figure 5.19: *Export the Bloom visualization to CSV/Excel*

1. Let's download the **Power BI Desktop** App from the Microsoft Store. The Microsoft Store enables us to download the application to our local computer, which makes the demonstration much easier to follow along:

Figure 5.20: *Install the Power BI application*

2. Next, you will need to import your relationship CSV file into Power BI:

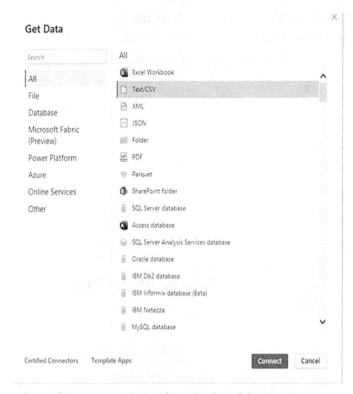

Figure 5.21: *Import relationship CSV/Excel file into Power BI*

Once the data is imported into Power BI, you will need to install the '`drill down graph`' visualization package. Here are the steps:

1. Click the ellipses to view more visualization options.

2. Select `Get more visuals` from the dropdown menu:

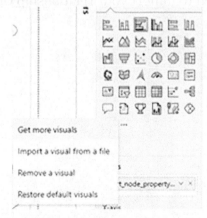

Figure 5.22: *Install the 'drill down graph' visualization package*

3. Once you click **Get more visuals**, you will see a search bar. Type **drill down graph** into the search bar and select the image, as shown:

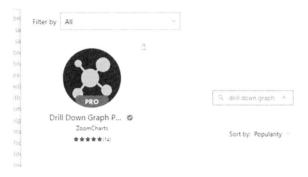

Figure 5.23: *Select the 'drill down graph' visualization package*

Now that you have the data and the drill down package in Power BI, you can proceed to create the graph visualization as well as leverage the drill down capabilities offered by Power BI.

Select the properties from the dataset in regard to which the column would indicate the source node, target node, and value of the relationship between the two nodes. In this case, we already have properties labeled **start_node_property** and **end_node_property**, so we can include these as the source node and target nodes:

Figure 5.24: *Include these properties as the Source Nodes, Target Nodes, and Values*

By including these columns as the source nodes and target nodes, we will see the graph visualization image appear, as shown in *Figure 5.25*. Power BI allows us to drill down on the graph by using other dashboard displays. In this case, we will use a bar chart to hone in on only `mexican cornbread` recipes as an example:

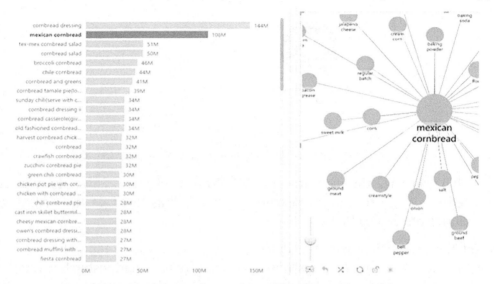

Figure 5.25: *Create the graph visualization accompanied*
by the drill down capabilities of Power BI

Conclusion

In this chapter, we explored various facets of Neo4j Bloom as a seamless integration business intelligence tool to interact with the Neo4j graph database. We began by setting up the Bloom browser, configuring the node and relationship styles, and proceeded to incorporate Cypher queries and Scene actions to maximize the usefulness of the tool as an exploratory data insights mechanism.

The chapter also focused on other features of Bloom, such as the export to CSV method, which enables us to export the results of our analysis and share them with others or import them into other visualization tools such as Power BI.

Moving beyond Bloom, the chapter also explored the integration of graph data with Power BI. We walked through the process of installing Power BI, importing data, and showcased the synergy between graph data and one of the most commonly used business intelligence tools on the market: Power BI.

In summary, this chapter has been a comprehensive walkthrough of the functionalities of both Neo4j Bloom and Power BI as exploratory mechanisms for graph data science. Graph visualizations play an important role in explaining to stakeholders the value and benefits gained by storing our data in a graph format.

In the next chapter, we will explore the relationship between the graph database and large language models (LLMs) as a way to enrich our existing graph data and push the boundaries of what is possible in extracting meaningful insights from our data.

Points to Remember

- **Utilize Cypher Queries and Scene Actions in Bloom**: We explored the incorporation of Cypher queries and Scene actions in Bloom, showcasing the tool's effectiveness and utility for exploratory graph analysis.

- **Export to CSV Feature**: A key feature in Bloom, export to CSV, was highlighted to showcase its ability to share results of the analysis as well as its compatibility with other visualization tools such as Power BI.

- **Integration with Power BI**: The integration of graph data with Power BI was explored to illustrate the opportunities to incorporate graph data science into the realm of business intelligence.

Enriching Neo4j Data with ChatGPT

Introduction

ChatGPT was first released by OpenAI in 2022. It is a large language model (LLM). Natural language processing (NLP) has been an important branch of data science for many years, and the development of ChatGPT is seen by many in the industry as an inflection point in the efficacy of NLP models.

While many other LLM models exist (such as Bard by Google) and many more are being developed as we speak, we will focus on ChatGPT for this chapter to illustrate how we can enrich existing data with these fantastic new tools and store the data in Neo4j.

Enriching data with ChatGPT has wide-reaching implications. In the era of data-driven decision-making, ChatGPT can help unlock untapped potential in the data. It has the capacity to understand your text prompts, generate new data, provide code to help you evaluate your data, augment text-based data, and many more capabilities as well. The ability to transform data opens new possibilities for many industries and research fields. For example, insights drawn from the enriched data could illuminate hidden patterns and correlations, contributing to more strategic decision-making.

Structure

In this chapter, we will cover the following topics:

- Learning the Basics of ChatGPT
- Importing a Neo4j Database into Neo4j Aura

- Exploratory Data Analysis of the Patent Dataset
- Enriching Data Using the ChatGPT API in Python
- Creating Embeddings of the Patent Summaries
- Reducing the Size of the Vector Embeddings to Visualize with Plotly in Python

Getting Started with ChatGPT

The easiest way to begin working with ChatGPT is to use the browser version: https://chat.openai.com/. Once logged in, type a message in the chat window and press *Enter*. ChatGPT will store your conversation so that you can pick up where you left off at a later date:

Figure 6.1: *Illustration of ChatGPT user interface*

As we can see in the response, we need to first request an API key from OpenAI. We could ask ChatGPT for steps on how to complete this as well. However, since ChatGPT was trained on data through the end of 2021, we sometimes need to supplement our search with Google/Bing search:

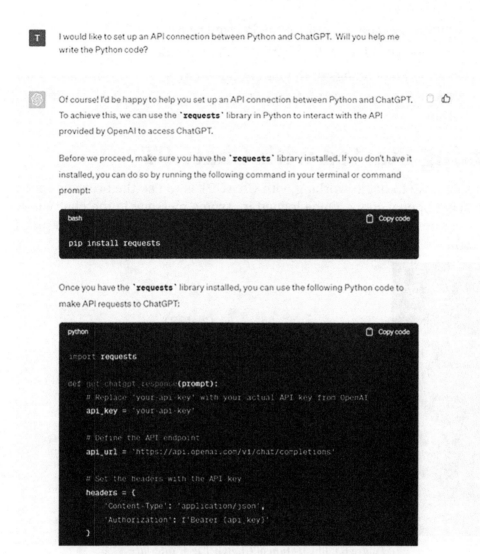

Figure 6.2: *Response from ChatGPT with API instructions*

To create a new secret key to communicate with ChatGPT directly from our Python Jupyter Notebook, navigate to the following link: https://platform. openai.com/account/api-keys. You may also need to sign up with payment for the API to work properly:

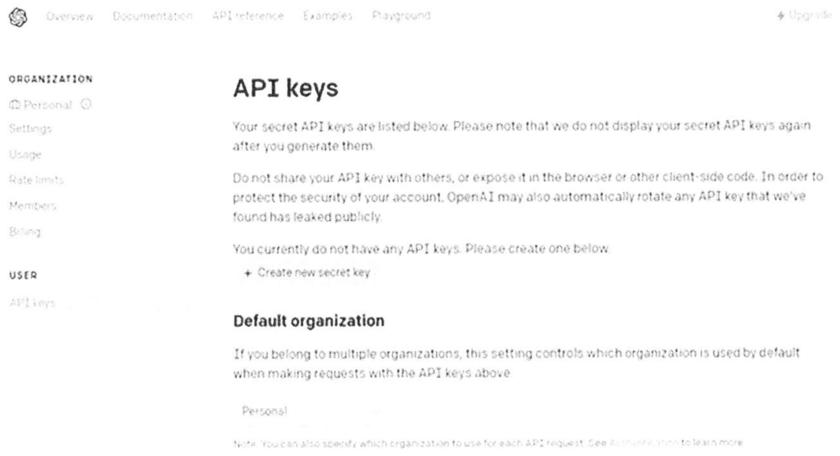

Figure 6.3: *Request a new secret key from OpenAI*

Once your key has been created, insert it into the following text block to connect to ChatGPT directly from Jupyter Notebook!

```
```

#pip install openai

import os

import openai

openai.api_key = "YOUR KEY" # you will need to add your own key here

openai.Model.list()
```
```

After a connection to ChatGPT has been established, insert any prompt and retrieve feedback from the LLM. More instructions and tutorials can be found at the following link: https://github.com/openai/openai-cookbook/blob/main/examples/How_to_format_inputs_to_ChatGPT_models.ipynb:

```
```

example with a system message

response = openai.ChatCompletion.create(

    model="gpt-3.5-turbo",

    messages=[

        {"role": "system", "content": "You are a helpful assistant."},

        {"role": "user", "content": "Explain the value of the Neo4j graph database to a teenager."},
```
```

```
    ],
    temperature=0,
)


print(response['choices'][0]['message']['content'])
```

When we run this code, we can view an output of the prompt directly in our Jupyter Notebook. This API flexibility allows us to later query Neo4j and request ChatGPT enrich the data we send:

```
# example with a system message
response = openai.ChatCompletion.create(
    model="gpt-3.5-turbo",
    messages=[
        {"role": "system", "content": "You are a helpful assistant."},
        {"role": "user", "content": "Explain the value of the Neo4j graph database to a teenager."},
    ],
    temperature=0,
)

print(response['choices'][0]['message']['content'])

Hey there! So, imagine you have a lot of information, like a bunch of puzzle pieces. Now, usually, you would try to organize th
ese pieces in a way that makes sense, right? Well, that's where Neo4j comes in!

Neo4j is like a special tool that helps you organize and connect all these puzzle pieces in a really cool way. Instead of just
putting them in a regular box, Neo4j lets you create a graph, kind of like a web of connections.

This graph database is super useful because it helps you see how different pieces of information are related to each other. I
t's like having a map that shows you all the connections between things. You can easily find patterns, understand complex relat
ionships, and discover new insights.

For example, let's say you're interested in movies. With Neo4j, you can see how actors, directors, and genres are all connecte
d. You can quickly find out which actors have worked together, which directors have made similar movies, or which genres are mo
st popular.

So, Neo4j is like a powerful tool that helps you make sense of lots of information by showing you how everything is connected.
It's like having a superpower to explore and understand complex relationships. Pretty cool, right?
```

Figure 6.4: Example ChatGPT API request

In the next section, we will import a database dump of US Patent data in order to prompt ChatGPT to help us enrich our data stored in Neo4j.

Importing the Database in Aura DB

For this illustration, we will import a Neo4j database dump provided by the following article: https://frodnar.github.io/posts/2023-09-30_building_llm_chatbot_neo4j/. Alternatively, you can navigate to the source files for this chapter of the book to download the file directly.

Next, follow the steps outlined in *Chapter 3, Importing Data into the Neo4j Graph Database*, to create an online Neo4j Aura DB account if you have not already done so. We will leverage this account to efficiently import the database dump file.

Click the white space of the following box once you have created an instance. This will navigate you to the screen to import a database:

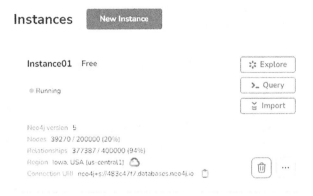

Figure 6.5: *Homescreen of Neo4j Aura DB*

Once we are within the database instance information pane, we must follow these steps:

1. Click the `Import Database` tab to navigate to the drop file box, illustrated as follows:

2. Drop the database dump file into the following box.

3. Select `Upload` once prompted to begin the import process:

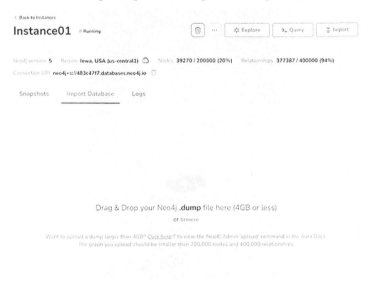

Figure 6.6: *Drop the database dump file into this location*

By following these steps, you will create a database of patents from the first half of 2023 representing 39,000 nodes and 377,000 relationships. We will explore the Patent database before we showcase how we can use ChatGPT to enrich the information in this database.

Exploratory Data Analysis (EDA) of the Patent Database

When exploring a new database, **exploratory data analysis (EDA)** is an important first step. In Neo4j, a natural starting point is to check the number of nodes and relationships, as well as the properties stored within the database. We can view this in the left pane of the Neo4j Browser window, where we can see there are 39,270 nodes and 377,387 relationships stored in the database:

***Figure 6.7**: View the summary information of the database*

Patents are a form of **intellectual property** (**IP**) used as a form of legal protection to investors for their original creations or innovations. The inventor is provided legal rights to the idea in exchange for publicly disclosing the details of the invention, which allows the broader community to learn from and build upon it after the patent's protection expires.

Patents are particularly intriguing as a graph data problem and in the context of **large language models** (**LLMs**) because the universe of patents is vast and interlinked. Each patent often cites prior patents and, in turn, is cited by subsequent patents. In addition, LLMs can help delve deeper into the content and context of the patents. Patent documents are dense, technical, and challenging to understand. Therefore, LLMs can assist in summarizing the information as well as creating embeddings of the documents by which we can draw similarities between the patents. For example, this patent (https://patents. google.com/patent/US20230000008A1/en?oq=US20230000008A1) provides the template used to create the Neo4j data model with various elements of the patent, including:

- **Assignee**: Typically the individual or entity that holds the ownership rights of the patent. This could be an individual, a company, or even a university.

- **Inventor**: The individual or group of individuals who conceived the original idea of the invention and are credited for the patent's innovative work.

- **Topic**: It refers to the specific subject or field of technology of the patent. This could range from pharmaceuticals, technology, mechanical devices, and more.

Let's write a few Cypher queries to better understand the database before we begin using ChatGPT to enrich our data. To begin, let's find out how many patent documents are in the database.

```
MATCH (a:Document) RETURN count(a) as Number_Documents
```

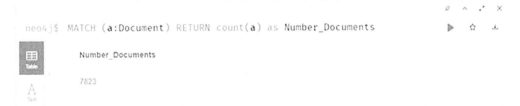

Figure 6.8: *Number of patents from the first half of 2023*

We are also interested to know which topics are most commonly covered by these patents. With the Cypher query given here, we can view the most common topic by the number of documents linked to each topic.

```
MATCH (a:Topic)<-[r:IS_IN]-(b:Document)
RETURN a.name as Topic_Name, count(b) as topic_count
ORDER BY topic_count DESC
LIMIT 5
```

By running this code, it is seen that the largest category of topics is for medical devices; 390 patents were awarded in the first half of 2023 in regard to this topic:

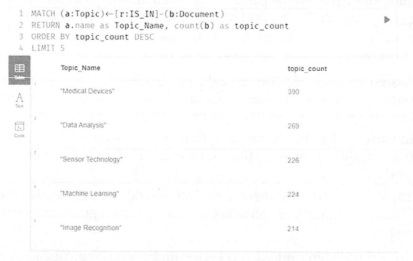

Figure 6.9: *Count the number of documents linked to each topic*

Once we know how many patents are awarded by topic, the next natural question to ask is who is filing these patents? In the next query, we search for the Assignees linked to the documents and return the results in descending order to view the Assignees with the most number of filed patents first:

```
MATCH (a:Document)-[r:ASSIGNED_TO]->(b:Assignee)
RETURN b.name as Assignee_Name, count(a) as document_count
ORDER BY document_count DESC
LIMIT 5
```

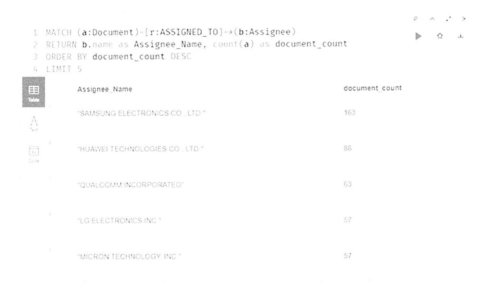

Figure 6.10: *Count the number of Assignees linked to each document*

In the next section, we will leverage this database to showcase how we can use ChatGPT to enrich the information in this database.

Enriching Neo4j Data with ChatGPT

First, you will need to connect to Aura DB as well as OpenAI via the API keys we created previously.

Once connected to Neo4j and OpenAI, we can pull all of the patents related to the topic of Machine Learning and enrich this data using ChatGPT. There are many avenues available by which ChatGPT could help enrich our data for this particular use case, including:

- Concise Patent Summaries
- Topic Expansion
- Profile of Investors
- Identify Similarities Between Patents

In this section, we will focus on the first bullet point, *Concise Patent Summaries*. *Patents* are lengthy and complex documents. Often, the patents use terms that are complex and confusing to the layman. Therefore, we can design a prompt to feed the patent documents to ChatGPT and request a concise summary of the patent. This will enable us to quickly understand the intent of the patent and help us further analyze and navigate the complex patent landscape.

By executing the following code in Python, we can pull the patent documents from Neo4j into a pandas dataframe related to topics of Machine Learning. If you are running this code using Jupyter Notebook, you will first need to connect to Aura DB. This code can be found in the code accompanying this chapter:

```
```

```
MATCH (c:Topic)<-[r2:IS_IN]-(a:Document)-[r:ASSIGNED_TO]->(b:Assignee)
WHERE c.name = 'Machine Learning'
RETURN id(a) as ida
, a.title as Patent_Title
, b.name as Patent_Owner
, a.abstract as Patent_Abstract
LIMIT 300
```

```
```

ida	Patent_Title	Patent_Owner	Patent_Abstract
4642	BEHAVIORAL THREAT DETECTION ENGINE	WEBROOT INC.	Examples of the present disclosure describe sy...
4781	METHOD AND SYSTEM FOR DETERMINING TASK COMPATI...	CONTINENTAL AUTOMOTIVE GMBH	The example embodiments relate to a computer-i...
4855	TECHNIQUES FOR VALIDATING FEATURES FOR MACHINE...	ARMIS SECURITY LTD.	A system and method for machine learning featu...
4712	MACHINE LEARNING RECOMMENDATION ENGINE FOR CON...	DROPBOX, INC.	A content management system obtains at least a...
4780	LSTM-BASED HOT-ROLLING ROLL-BENDING FORCE PRED...	NORTHEASTERN UNIVERSITY	Provided is an LSTM-based hot-rolling roll-ben...

Figure 6.11: *Machine Learning Patents*

We now need to send this data to ChatGPT via the API to request a short description of the Patent so that we can append the information to our dataframe. In the following code, we send each of the patent abstracts to ChatGPT via the API and ask ChatGPT to "summarize the following patent abstract in laymen's terms in fewer than 100 tokens."

```
```

```python
def summarize_abstract(abstract_text):
    response = openai.Completion.create(
        model="text-davinci-002",
        prompt=f"Summarize the following patent abstract in laymen's
terms in fewer than 100 tokens: {abstract_text}",
        max_tokens=100
    )
```

```
    return response.choices[0].text.strip()


# Loop through the dataframe and apply the summary function
df['Summary'] = df['Patent_Abstract'].apply(summarize_abstract)


# Display the updated dataframe with summaries
display(df.head())
```
```

As we can see in the output of the dataframe with the newly appended Summary
column, ChatGPT has provided a concise summary of each patent's description,
making it more accessible for the average reader. Patent attorneys often employ
technical terminology, so having a simplified version is certainly beneficial:

| | ids | Patent_Title | Patent_Owner | Patent_Abstract | Summary |
|---|---|---|---|---|---|
| 0 | 4642 | BEHAVIORAL THREAT DETECTION ENGINE | WEBROOT INC | Examples of the present disclosure describe systems and methods for a behavioral threat detection engine In examples, the behavioral threat detection engine manages execution of one or more virtual machines, wherein each virtual machine processes a rule in relation to a context The behavioral threat detection engine uses any of a variety of techniques to identify when events occur Accordingly, the behavioral threat detection engine provides event indications, in the form of event packets, to one or more virtual machines, such that corresponding rules are able to process the events accordingly Eventually, a rule may make a determination as to the presence or absence of a behavior As a result, execution of the associated virtual machine may be halted, thereby indicating to the behavioral threat detection engine that a determination has been made Thus a behavioral threat detection engine employs a behavior-based approach to detecting malicious or potentially malicious behaviors | The present disclosure describes systems and methods for a behavioral threat detection engine The behavioral threat detection engine manages execution of one or more virtual machines Each virtual machine processes a rule in relation to a context The behavioral threat detection engine uses any of a variety of techniques to identify when events occur The behavioral threat detection engine provides event indications to one or more virtual machines, such that corresponding rules are able to process the events Eventually, a rule may make a determination as to the presence or absence |

*Figure 6.12: Summary of patents appended to the dataframe*

We can now write these summaries back to Neo4j in the form of a new property
on the Document node. Since the data is stored as a pandas dataframe, we can
leverage the methods outlined in *Chapter 3, Importing Data into the Neo4j Graph
Database*, to load this data into Neo4j directly from Python:

```
```
# Update node summary
def update_node_summary(session, node_id, summary):
    query = """
    MATCH (a:Document)
    WHERE id(a) = $node_id
```

```
    SET a.Summary = $summary
    """"

    session.run(query, node_id=node_id, summary=summary)


# Loop through DataFrame and update each node
with driver.session() as session:
    for index, row in df.iterrows():
        node_id = row['ida']
        summary = row['Summary']
        update_node_summary(session, node_id, summary)


driver.close()
```

In the next section, we will query these Summary properties from the Document nodes, use ChatGPT to help us create vector representations of the summaries, and then visualize the patents using the Python package, plotly.

Creating Embeddings of the Patent Summaries

Let us dive deeper into the transformations we can apply to complex patent data by integrating large language models (LLMs) like ChatGPT with our Neo4j database. Instead of sifting through lengthy summaries of patents, we can now use embeddings to represent the text in a condensed, numeric representation. Embeddings capture the essence and semantic meaning of the text documents while providing a streamlined way to analyze vast volumes of data.

Embeddings are a way to condense vast amounts of information and are used often to condense text in the field of natural language processing. While the list of numbers that result from an embedding might not make much sense to look at, they hold the essence of the original information by leveraging artificial intelligence, specifically deep neural networks, to learn the best representation of the data structure.

The following code takes a list of summaries we created in the last section, processes each summary using the OpenAI's "ada" model to obtain an embedding (or vector representation), and then collects and displays the embeddings:

```
```

embeddings = OpenAIEmbeddings(openai_api_key=openai_api_key, model_
name="ada")

embeddings_list = []

for summary in df['Summary']:
    embeddings_list.append(embeddings.embed_query(summary))

print(embeddings_list)
```
```

The embeddings are lists of numbers that contain the context of the text document. As you can see, in the following figure, this vector is neither readable to humans nor does it reveal stories of explicit information. However, beneath the layer of numbers are multiple layers of rich meaning and context:

Summary	Summary_Embeddings
The present disclosure describes systems and methods for a behavioral threat detection engine. The behavioral threat detection engine manages execution of one or more virtual	[-0.061152393007540926, -0.015168556483798452, 0.006146453134689828, -0.0024838179062750734, -0.014012983575432807, 0.03195757322012071, -0.02024245200794006, -0.011701837758701514, -0.015128708917328678, -0.007903056911012332, 0.001043502326161314, 0.02959329545211796, 0.005136987038724144, 0.0053827123016372685, 0.0076042020251341136, 0.013587944729066968, 0.030655891636710012, -0.005847598248811609, 0.0072854228903597345, 0.003142959343005747, 0.019153290779034826, 0.0040743913197933655, -0.017771915925329666, -0.006813896147768371, -0.023138025074271196, -0.00627595679439405, 0.030523066415144094, -0.03445467248439919, -0.020999552045575597, 0.008500767614091315, 0.0017034740369420928, -0.018542298485121796, -0.004735193071793613, 0.005459086338376397, -0.0054657275994546934, 0.02511710969973279, 0.013986418531119624, 0.005887445349620111

Figure 6.13: Embedding of the summary text

The OpenAI model can interpret this vector and allow for question answering, similarity matching, and many more powerful analytics. The capabilities go beyond merely interpreting the text. In the next section, we will use a dimensionality reduction technique to visualize communities of patent documents.

Reducing the Dimension of Embeddings

It is often said that a picture is worth a thousand words. Visualizing complex data, such as high-dimensional vectors, can be a rewarding method to explore and analyze the data. However, embeddings are not well suited for visualization, given their high dimensionality. Therefore, we often need to reduce the vectors from thousands of dimensions to only two for our human brains to interpret the similarities between our data points.

This section explores a form of dimensionality reduction of the high-dimensional vectors into a 2D or 3D space using a method called **principal component analysis (PCA)**. PCA is a linear transformation technique that seeks to project the original data into a new coordinate system, which we can then plot in a chart.

Before we run PCA, we are going to first create communities of the embeddings using the algorithm, K-means. K-means is one of the more commonly used clustering algorithms, known for its simplicity and efficiency. For embeddings, K-means can be particularly useful. Given that embeddings are high-dimensional vectors, clustering these vectors allows us to discover inherent groupings or communities within the data. The following code enables us to create five communities of patents based on their embeddings:

```
n_clusters = 5
kmeans = KMeans(n_clusters=n_clusters, random_state=42)
df['community'] = kmeans.fit_predict(embeddings_list)
```

Now that we have communities added to our dataset, we continue forward with running our dimensionality reduction using PCA with the following code:

```
pca = PCA(n_components=2)
reduced_embeddings = pca.fit_transform(embeddings_list)
```

Once the dataset has been reduced in terms of dimensions, we can now visualize the patents using the plotly package. We can use the following code to create a scatter plot based on the new dataset after running PCA:

```
```
# Create a dataframe from the reduced embeddings
df_embeddings = pd.DataFrame(reduced_embeddings, columns=['x', 'y'])
df_embeddings['community'] = df['community']

# Plot using Plotly
fig = px.scatter(df_embeddings, x='x', y='y', color='community', title="2D
PCA of Embeddings", color_continuous_scale=px.colors.sequential.Viridis)
fig.show()
```
```

This code generates the following scatter plot. The colors represent the K-means communities of the original embeddings:

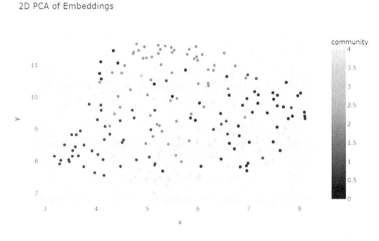

Figure 6.14: Visualization of embeddings of the patent summaries

This figure represents a snapshot of our embedded data in a way that enables us to draw more insights than the raw, lengthy embeddings. At first glance, the chart may appear complicated, but it's this density and clustering of points that is illuminating.

Conclusion

In our journey to make patent data more accessible, we integrated ChatGPT to provide a concise and layperson-friendly summary. We transformed these simplified texts further by generating numerical vectors, or embeddings, that encapsulate the patents' content.

Once we transitioned from text to numerical embeddings, we touched upon the numerous analytical possibilities. First, we implemented K-means clustering to group similar patents together. Next, we utilized PCA to reduce the embeddings into a format that enables us to view the data in a 2D plot.

Combining the power of ChatGPT's textual intelligence with the flexibility and power of Neo4j opens many avenues for future work and analytics. In the next chapter, *Chapter 7, Neo4j Vector Index and Retrieval-Augmented Generation (RAG)*, we will continue on this path of leveraging ChatGPT alongside Neo4j by illustrating how we can use Neo4j vector storage to scale the storage of our embeddings, as well as the analytics we can implement on top of these embeddings.

Points to Remember

- **ChatGPT Enrichment:** ChatGPT allows us to simplify complex jargon-filled patent data into clear and meaningful summaries.

- **Embeddings and Vectors:** Textual summaries and other complex data representations can be transformed into numerical vectors called embeddings. These embeddings enable advanced analytics not possible on raw text files.

- **Dimensionality Reduction with PCA:** Principal Component Analysis (PCA) is a technique used to simplify the complexities of a multi-dimensional embedding. By reducing the dimensions, we distill the data structure into something easier to understand.

- **Community Detection using K-means:** We clustered the embeddings using the k-means clustering approach to identify groups or communities of patents. These clusters hint at shared themes or patterns within the patent text.

- **Visualization with Plotly:** An effective visualization strengthens the analysis as stated in the common phrase "*a picture paints a thousand words.*" Using the plotly library, we were able to craft a dynamic visualization of the patent embeddings.

Neo4j Vector Index and Retrieval-Augmented Generation (RAG)

Introduction

The Retrieval-Augmented Generation (RAG) model is an innovative approach in natural language processing (NLP) that combines the strengths of large-scale information retrieval with powerful language generation capabilities. RAG retrieves relevant document snippets from text corpuses/text documents and leverages these snippets to generate contextually relevant outputs. RAG can significantly reduce the common issue of "*hallucinations*" or incorrect responses from an LLM. By grounding the LLM generation process in retrieved information that is contextually relevant, RAG helps ensure that the outputs are contextually accurate.

With a scalable database solution like Neo4j, we can now run the RAG models using vector embeddings, similar to those we discussed in the previous chapter, to store the semantic essence of the data in a high-dimensional space. This ability enables us to search the vector space for similar items in an efficient way, transforming the analysis from large text documents into new context-aware, intricate connections between documents.

In an effort to discover knowledge from text documents, why not use a knowledge graph like Neo4j to optimize our search? Let's explore it.

Structure

In this chapter, we will cover the following topics:

- Creating the Neo4j Vector Index
- Preparing the Stock Market Text Data for Vector Embeddings
- Creating and Storing the Embeddings in Neo4j
- Enriching the Knowledge Graph from the Embeddings

Neo4j Vector Indexing

Vector indexes represent a special type of indexing designed to facilitate efficient searches within high-dimensional data spaces. In traditional databases, indexes help speed up the search through the use of keys or attributes. However, as data becomes more complex, the traditional indexing method often falls short.

Vector indexes enable us to search the spatial relationships of the vectors and search for ranges of similarity within the high-dimensional space. Since the data is stored within a database, we do not face some of the common hurdles of attempting to store too much data on the computer all at once. Instead, we can offload this complex processing to the database and retrieve only the relevant documents. The scalability of the Neo4j database combined with its support for real-time applications makes the storage of vector embeddings a game changer for applications relying on retrieval of large, complex information in real-time (for example, fraud detection, recommendation systems).

Furthermore, we can integrate the vector queries seamlessly into our graph model. This enables us to traverse not only all the relevant text documents but also search the knowledge graph in a unified and seamless integration.

Data Preparation for Vector Embeddings

For the next exercise, we will utilize publicly available information for the company, Tesla. Tesla manufactures electric vehicles and is traded on the New York Stock Exchange. Because the stock is publicly traded, the company is required to file an annual report called a 10-K to inform shareholders about significant updates within the company as well as financial information.

Our first step will involve creating segments from the report and then embedding each segment to save in Neo4j. As we discussed in the previous chapter, embeddings offer us the ability to store large amounts of text data in a computer-readable format, which also preserves the semantic meaning of the text. By embedding the 10-K sections as vectors, we will be able to connect the themes of the 10-K with other pertinent information about the company within the knowledge graph.

The U.S. Securities and Exchange Commission (SEC) provides an API that we can use to ingest the information from the 10-K. Follow the reference code for this chapter to pull the full overview from Tesla's 10-K.

```
```
URL of Tesla's 10-K filing
filing_10_k_url =
'https://www.sec.gov/Archives/edgar/data/1318605/000156459021004599/tsla
-10k_20201231.htm'

# extract text section "Item 1 - Business" from 10-K
item_1_text = extractorApi.get_section(filing_10_k_url, '1', 'text')
```
```

This code snippet will extract the initial overview from the large 10-K document. The output appears something like this:

```
ITEM 1.

BUSINESS

##TABLE_END

Overview

We design, develop, manufacture, sell and lease
high-performance fully electric vehicles and energy generation and storage syst
ems, and offer
services related to our sustainable energy products. We generally sell our prod
ucts directly to
customers, including through our website and retail locations. We also continue
to grow our
customer-facing infrastructure through a global network of vehicle service cent
ers, Mobile Service
technicians, body shops, Supercharger stations and Destination Chargers to acce
lerate the widespread
adoption of our products. We emphasize performance, attractive styling and the
safety of our users
and workforce in the design and manufacture of our products and are continuing
to develop full
self-driving technology for improved safety. We also strive to lower the cost o
f ownership for our
customers through continuous efforts to reduce manufacturing costs and by offer
ing financial
```

Figure 7.1: *Overview of Tesla from the 10-K*

As we can see, the API provided by the SEC enables us to quickly and easily pull in relevant information for our company of interest. This is a crucial first step in our analysis of company embeddings because it streamlines the process of retrieving relevant and timely information about the company.

Next, we need to create a vector index to store the embeddings once they are created. We can use the following Cypher command to create the index:

```
` ` `

graph.query("""
CALL db.index.vector.createNodeIndex(
    'TeslaEmbeddings', //index name
    'Chunk', //node label
    'tesla_embedding', //property name
    1536, //vector size
    'cosine' //similarity metric
)
""")

` ` `
```

This code creates a new index called `TeslaEmbeddings` in a node labeled Chunk (as in text-chunks). The vector size depends on the embedding you intend to use. The embedding we use from OpenAI is of length 1536.

Cosine similarity is a similarity metric often used in NLP and is the similarity metric we will use here for our embedding analysis. Cosine similarity measures the similarity between two vectors by calculating the angle between two vectors projected in a high dimensional space. Mathematically, cosine similarity is computed by first taking the dot product of the two vectors, summing the products of the corresponding entries in the two sequences of numbers, and then dividing this by the product of the magnitude (or length of the vector line) of both vectors. The resulting calculation ranges from -1 (meaning exactly opposite vectors) to 1 (exactly the same). In text analysis, cosine similarity is useful because it is not influenced by the length of the text but, instead, by the angle between the two vectors. This way, if one document has a much longer length than the other document, the similarity can still be similar if the words used are similar.

We need to split our text document into smaller chunks in order to pass the information through the OpenAI API in an efficient way. Therefore, we will use the following code to split/chunk the text using the `LangChain` library, which is a commonly used framework for NLP and LLM applications:

```
```
text_splitter = CharacterTextSplitter(chunk_size=2000, chunk_overlap=20)
docs = text_splitter.split_documents(combined_docs)
```
```

The `chunk_size` is a parameter used to determine the length of the tokens passed within each chunk. The `chunk_overlap` parameter enables us to allow a small amount of overlap between chunks to preserve some of the context from one chunk to the next. While chunk overlap may lead to redundancy or inefficiency in processing, it is often considered worthwhile to preserve the context of the document.

Storing the Data in Neo4j as a Vector Embedding

With the vector index created and the document stored in chunks, we can now run the following code to create embeddings of each of these chunks and store each chunk embedding as its own node in Neo4j:

```
```
hybrid_db = Neo4jVector.from_documents(
    docs,
    OpenAIEmbeddings(),
    url=url,
    username=username,
    password=password,
    index_name = "TeslaEmbeddings",
    search_type="hybrid"
)
```
```

This code will run each chunk stored in the docs variable through the OpenAI embedding model and store the resulting embedding in Neo4j using the index we created called `TeslaEmbeddings`. The following figure illustrates the result in Neo4j:

Figure 7.2: *Illustrate embeddings stored in Neo4j*

The embedding as well as the text from the associated chunk are each stored on the node in Neo4j. This capability to store embeddings in a native graph database opens many new doors for our analytics. For example, we can now build applications that search not only for classic knowledge graph contextual information but also high-dimensional embeddings that densely represent a wealth of information.

For example, we can ask questions directly of these embeddings and store the results of our queries back to the knowledge graph. Let's next ask a question of the embeddings: What are the topics covered in these documents?

```
print(qa({"question": "What are the topics covered in these documents?"})["answer"])

The documents cover the following topics:

1. Legal proceedings and potential penalties related to environmental regulations.
2. Overview of Tesla's business, including the design, development, manufacturing, and sales of electric vehicles and energy generation and storage systems.
3. Segment information, including the automotive segment and the energy generation and storage segment.
4. The use, storage, and disposal of lithium-ion battery packs and ongoing regulatory changes.
5. Regulations applicable to solar and battery storage providers, including interconnection agreements with utilities.
6. Net metering and its availability to solar customers in most states in the U.S.
7. Competition in the automotive market.
```

Figure 7.3: *Return Embeddings stored in Neo4j using Python API*

When we send the preceding query to OpenAI, it first embeds the question itself and then runs a cosine similarity search to return the relevant information from the embeddings. Let's take a moment to pause and reflect on how incredible it is that this capability exists. In other words, we can store a list of numbers in a database, ask the database a question, and GPT will return to us the information requested without requiring us to ever read the document. Wow!

Enriching the Knowledge Graph from the Embeddings

We can request GPT to summarize each of the seven sections outlined in the previous section and then write this summarized information back to the Neo4j knowledge graph. Instead of reading each of the sections, we can offload the work to GPT and store the results in a meaningful way at scale:

```
regulatory = qa({"question": "Which regulatory impacts and changes are discussed?"})["answer"]
print(regulatory)

The documents discuss several regulatory impacts and changes, including:

1. Compliance with federal laws administered by NHTSA: The company is required to comply with various federal laws, such as CAF
E standards, Theft Prevention Act requirements, consumer information labeling requirements, Early Warning Reporting requirement
s, and more.

2. Disclosure requirements: The U.S. Automobile Information and Disclosure Act requires manufacturers to disclose certain infor
mation regarding the manufacturer's suggested retail price, optional equipment and pricing. Fuel economy ratings and safety rat
ings are also required to be included.

3. Foreign regulations: Vehicles sold outside of the U.S. are subject to foreign safety, environmental, and other regulations.
These regulations may differ from those in the U.S. and may require redesign and retesting of vehicles.

4. European Union regulations: The European Union has established new rules regarding additional compliance oversight, which co
mmenced in 2020. There is also regulatory uncertainty related to the United Kingdom's withdrawal from the European Union.

5. Self-driving vehicle regulations: Laws pertaining to self-driving vehicles are evolving globally. While there are currently
no federal U.S. regulations specifically pertaining to self-driving vehicles, NHTSA has published recommended guidelines. Certa
in U.S. states have legal restrictions on self-driving vehicles, and other states are considering them. Similar restrictions an
d regulations exist in other markets, such as those following the regulations of the United Nations Economic Commission for Eur
ope and China.

6. Environmental regulations: The company has received notices of violation from the Bay Area Air Quality Management District r
elating to air permitting and compliance for the Fremont Factory. The company is in communication with the district and does no
t expect a material adverse impact on its business. Additionally, the German Umweltbundesamt has issued a notice and fine to th
e company's subsidiary in Germany for alleged non-compliance with applicable laws relating to end-of-life battery products. The
outcome of this matter is uncertain, but it is not expected to have a material adverse impact on the business.

7. EPA compliance: The company has received a follow-up information request from the EPA regarding the compliance of its Fremon
t Factory operations with applicable requirements under the Clean Air Act. The outcome of this matter is uncertain, but it is n
ot currently expected to have a material adverse impact on the business.
```

Figure 7.4: *Query specific information from the Embeddings stored in Neo4j*

In this example of one of the categories of text identified by GPT, we can see that Tesla currently faces seven distinct regulatory challenges. Regulatory risks are important considerations when attempting to quantify the value of a company. However, these risks are often complex for shareholders to understand. The GPT output above simplifies the text into a more digestible summary of the risks.

After we synthesize the information from each of the categories identified by the GPT AI model, we can write these summaries back to the knowledge graph. When analyzing complicated subjects like stock valuations, it is important to store as much information as possible in a flexible manner for simple retrieval. Therefore, we will link each of these topics directly to the company node, Tesla:

```
```

```
q = f""""""
MATCH (t:Company)
WHERE t.company_name = 'Tesla'
WITH t

MERGE (RegulatoryImpacts:RegulatoryImpacts)
WITH RegulatoryImpacts, t

MERGE (RegulatoryImpacts)<-[l:REGULATORY_IMPACTS {{description:
"{regulatory}"}}]-(t)
RETURN count(l)


""""""

graph.query(q)
```

```
```

With this code, we created a new node (if it does not already exist in the database) called `RegulatoryImpacts` by using the `MERGE` command. Once the new node is created, we then create a new relationship between `RegulatoryImpacts` and the company node. This new relationship is called `REGULATORY_IMPACTS`. It stores the regulatory impact summary from GPT in a property called `description`.

We created the following relationships for the Tesla company:

- `BUSIENSS_OVERVIEW`
- `LEGAL_DESCRIPTION`
- `REGULATORY_IMPACTS`
- `COMPETITION_INFORMATION`

With the following Cypher query, we can return the synthesized information from GPT from the Neo4j database:

```
```
```
MATCH (t:Company)-[r:BUSIENSS_OVERVIEW|LEGAL_DESCRIPTION|REGULATORY_
IMPACTS|COMPETITION_INFORMATION]->(a)
WHERE t.company_name = 'Tesla'
RETURN *
```
```
```

This query first anchors on the company node where the company name is Tesla. Next, the query follows the aforementioned four relationships to the associated nodes and returns all information. If we designed to change the architecture to split each of the components identified by GPT into separate nodes, then this query would still return all relevant information. For example, rather than storing the seven regulatory impacts on the relationship from Tesla to the `RegulatoryImpacts` node, we could have saved each impact as a separate node linked by the `REGULATORY_IMPACTS` relationship. It is a design preference, and the correct architecture depends on the business use-case and domain.

Once we run this query, we can see the following information appear in the Neo4j Browser:

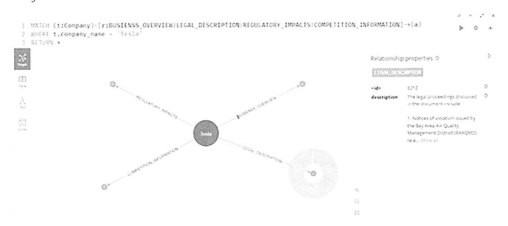

Figure 7.5: *Illustration of the Tesla Query Response in Neo4j*

The description produced by GPT is stored on the relationship in this particular architecture. We can also join the Tesla node to all of its associated embeddings by including the EMBEDDING relationship in the previous query. In this particular example, there are 25 embeddings connected to Tesla, which were used to create the descriptions illustrated above.

Semantic Search App with `Streamlit`

In this section, we will use the popular Python library, `Streamlit`, to create a front-end user interface for semantic search. `Streamlit` offers a straightforward framework, allowing for the rapid development of web applications.

With our foundational understanding of the capabilities of LLMs for semantic search, we can apply this expertise in a real-world example using movie data. The movie dataset included in the repository material for this chapter represents more than 20,000 movies as well as their descriptions. By applying our search query criteria in the '`Persona Description`' text box, we can execute the application to return the nearest matches:

Figure 7.6: *Semantic search app for movie recommendations*

In order to run this app, you will need to first install all the required dependencies, including the `Streamlit` library. We will then need to open a Terminal to execute the following simple command to run the Python script, which is stored in the code repository for this chapter:

```
streamlit run text_column_semantic_search_20240122.py
```

Once you run this command in the terminal, you will see the Streamlit app appear. From here, simply insert your OpenAI API key as well as the description of the movie you would like to watch, and then drag and drop the Excel file into the input box.

This program looks for a column in the CSV/Excel file called 'text' as the body of text to embed. You can upload anybody of text into this app as long as it has a column named 'text', and this app will provide a score of the rows that most closely match the provided persona. Alternatively, you can adjust the code to read a different column of your table if there is a different name such as 'description'.

Once you click the '**Run**' button, you will see a dataframe, similar to the one below, appears. This dataframe is sorted by the closest match by score. The app will embed each row of your dataframe, as well as the provided persona, and then it will run a cosine similarity search and provide a column, 'Score', to review the results:

movie_name	budget	popularity	runtime	tag_line	text	Score
Hercules	0	1.5676	98	The Legend Lives!	The film is an odd retelling of the story of Hercules battling the wizard Minos, who use...	0.3772
Up, Up, and Away	0	3.1123	90	0	A boy is the only family member without superpowers in this Disney Film. The world...	0.3673
Your Highness	49,900,000	5.6736	102	Get your quest on.	A fantasy movie about an arrogant, lazy prince and his more heroic brother who mus...	0.3663
Man of Steel	225,000,000	18.5388	143	You will believe that a man can fly.	A young boy learns that he has extraordinary powers and is not of this earth. As a you...	0.3662
Outcast	25,000,000	9.0296	98	To save their souls they must save a kingdom.	A mysterious warrior teams up with the daughter and son of a deposed Chinese Emp...	0.362
Master of the World	0	1.8263	102	The fabulous adventures of the man who conque	A mad genius tries to bomb the world into peace... The fabulous adventures of the m...	0.362
Deigo	40,000,000	2.9158	94	0	In a divided land, it takes a rebellious boy and his clandestine love for a Princess of an...	0.3581
The Blade Master	0	3.1696	92	Warrior. Magician. Hero. Thief. They called him.	Muscle-bound Ator and his mute Asian sidekick travel from the ends of the Earth to s...	0.3567
Yeelen	0	1.3227	105	0	A young man with magical powers journeys to his uncle to request help in fighting his...	0.3565
Spriggan	0	2.8638	90	0	An elite superhuman agent must stop a foreign military unit from seizing control of an...	0.3563
Tom and Jerry: The N...	0	10.978	84	0	The popular cartoon cat and mouse are thrown into a feature film. The story has the t...	0.3554

Figure 7.7: Output of semantic search app for movie recommendations

As you can see in the results from our prompt, Hercules is the movie that most closely matches the provided persona: "*Animated action movie where the hero saves the world.*" The Streamlit library offers an excellent user interface to explore and experiment with semantic search using OpenAI embeddings.

This demonstration showcases the capabilities of modern AI and NLP techniques as well as enables us to discover and explore future advancements to this capability by coupling these results with attributes from knowledge graphs.

Conclusion

In this chapter, we harnessed the power of AI for enhanced knowledge discovery. It is worth taking a moment to reflect on the transformative capabilities that modern AI, particularly GPT models, bring to knowledge graph retrieval and data analysis. What we covered in this chapter is not just a technical accomplishment but a leap into the future where massive text documents become effortlessly navigable.

By embedding questions and using cosine similarity searches within a database, we bypass the traditional processes of information retrieval, which can be slow and inaccurate. The ability to ask a database a question and receive precise information in return is astounding.

Writing the information gathered from GPT back to Neo4j elevates the quality of insights we can derive from our data. It enables us to scale our analysis and pull in thousands of companies' information and assess commonalities, strengths, and weaknesses in new ways.

We also took a dive into using Streamlit as a front-end visualization tool to showcase the power of these embeddings using a movie dataset. Streamlit is a powerful Python package to help us iterate and explore the results of our experiments.

By harnessing GPT's embedding and enrichment in Neo4j's knowledge graph, we stand at the cusp of a revolution in data analytics. The heavy lifting of analysis is offloaded to AI, enabling humans to engage with the synthesized knowledge in an accurate and actionable way.

In the next chapter, we will explore some of the built-in algorithms that are available within Neo4j. In-database analytics supercharge our analysis by providing the analytical tools we need to apply to our data without transferring the data out of the database into a separate compute environment.

Points to Remember

- **Neo4j Vector Index:** The new Neo4j Vector Index enables us to store embeddings and efficiently run similarity searches.
- **Chunking the Data:** In NLP tasks, it is often necessary to chunk the text into manageable portions. The chunk overlap enables us to preserve context across the chunks.
- **Creating and Storing the Embeddings:** We transformed the text into numerical representations of their structure using GPT to be retrieved by the AI system.
- **Deep Insights and Scaling the Analysis:** The summarization and enrichment capabilities of GPT allow for scaling the analysis across large sets of data by combining with the flexible and powerful storage of Neo4j.
- **Streamlit for Data Exploration:** Streamlit is a powerful Python library to create front-end visualizations. We used the library to explore the movie recommendations using the OpenAI embeddings.

Graph Algorithms in Neo4j

Introduction

As data becomes increasingly connected, graph algorithms play a large role in helping extract meaning from the data. Knowledge graphs offer a unique opportunity to navigate and understand the intricate web of interconnected data. Specifically, Neo4j offers the unique opportunity to run graph algorithms directly in the database.

Graph algorithms are the backbone of complex network analysis tackling problems such as node centrality, community detection, shortest path, and graph embeddings with neural networks. Graph algorithms open the door to many possibilities for complex analysis.

By the end of this chapter, you will have an understanding of how graph algorithms within Neo4j can be used to transform data into actionable insights.

Structure

In this chapter, we will cover the following types of algorithms:

- Centrality
- Community Detection
- Similarity
- Link Prediction
- Network Embeddings and Graph Neural Network

Centrality

Centrality algorithms play a pivotal role in graph data science as they are intended to help unravel the nodes which are most pivotal, influential, and/or important within the network. As a concrete example, we see centrality algorithms at work on social media platforms where the most heavily followed *"influencers"* are pushed to the top of the news feed. These influential nodes are discovered using a variety of centrality measures.

PageRank

The PageRank algorithm was initially developed by Google co-founders Larry Page and Sergey Brin. It is a centrality measure that revolutionized web search algorithms. Its premise is elegant yet powerful, which is to measure the importance of nodes (for example, webpages) in a network (for example, the World Wide Web) based on the connections between them.

A relationship from a highly ranked node to another node boosts the rank of the new node. The algorithm iteratively calculates the scores between node connections. The algorithm also incorporates a damping factor to reduce the randomness of connections, as well as to ensure all pages contain a non-zero rank.

To start, we must first create the cypher projection as follows:

```
MATCH (source:Recipe)-[:USES]->(target:Ingredient)
WHERE source.Recipe_Title CONTAINS 'cornbread'
WITH gds.graph.project('ingredients', source, target) AS g
RETURN
  g.graphName AS graph, g.nodeCount AS nodes, g.relationshipCount AS rels
```

This projects the Recipe to Ingredient relationship for all the cornbread recipes. We could remove the cornbread constraint, but this helps limit the size of our projection. The projection moves the data from the database to an in-memory location optimized for our graph analysis and will help us determine which ingredients are most important within the cornbread recipes.

Next, we can run the pageRank algorithm as follows:

```
CALL gds.pageRank.write('ingredients', { writeProperty: 'pageRank' })
```

The syntax in Neo4j **graph data science** (**GDS**) is straightforward. We specify the name of the projection, "ingredients", as well as the algorithm we would like to use. We then write the results of the algorithm back to the ingredient nodes in a property appropriately named 'pageRank.' We can then view the newly written property within the Neo4j Browser:

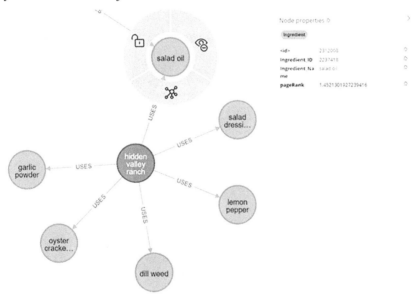

Figure 8.1: *Illustration of the pageRank property stored in the database*

Finally, we can write a cypher query to determine the most influential ingredients across the cornbread recipes:

```
MATCH (r:Recipe)-[:USES]->(i:Ingredient)
WHERE r.Recipe_Title CONTAINS 'cornbread'
WITH DISTINCT i
RETURN i.Ingredient_Name AS Ingredient, i.pageRank AS PageRank
ORDER BY i.pageRank DESC
LIMIT 10
```

This query returns the top 10 most influential ingredients in the cornbread recipes based on the `pageRank` algorithm. As you can see, eggs are the most important ingredient to consider when making cornbread:

Ingredient	PageRank
eggs	54.182461
salt	46.786139
onion	38.607501
milk	28.057664
sugar	24.776241
baking powder	24.219077
flour	20.145594
egg	18.830970
buttermilk	16.750039
butter	15.792249

Figure 8.2: Top 10 most influential ingredients in the cornbread recipes

As we can see, eggs are the most important ingredient in cornbread recipes, followed by salt and onion.

Node centrality can be a powerful tool to hone in on the most important elements of the graph. In tackling graph-related challenges, identifying key nodes is often a primary objective. This metric guides us to pivotal elements of the network's functionality.

Community Detection

Community detection helps us decipher the modular structure of a graph. Communities are clusters within a network. We can set the parameters to determine if the clusters should be more or less densely connected.

Whether we are mapping social interactions, unraveling complex biological systems, or parsing complex fraud networks, community detection helps us to identify subgroups with strong internal connections.

Louvain Hierarchical Clustering

Louvain is a highly efficient and widely used method for community detection within large networks. Louvain seeks to optimize a metric called modularity. Modularity is a scale value to measure the strength of the division of a network into modules or communities. Unlike clustering methods like k-means clustering, hierarchical clustering creates a tree of clusters called a dendrogram. This method can be particularly useful in understanding the data structure and identifying meaningful groupings within your data.

Louvain works in two phases. First, it assigns nodes to a community. Next, it aggregates nodes of the same community and builds a new network of communities until the modularity cannot be further increased.

We will use the same graph projection used in the previous section for cornbread node centrality. Once we run Louvain on this projection, we will see communities of cornbread recipes emerge. Let's run this code to write the **louvain** communities to the recipe and ingredient nodes:

```
CALL gds.louvain.write('ingredients', { writeProperty: 'louvainCommunity' })
YIELD communityCount, modularity, modularities
```

With this code block, we can capture the structure of the cornbread graph. Once we have these communities written to each node, we can simply aggregate the nodes to discover the largest communities using this approach:

```
MATCH (r:Recipe)
WHERE r.louvainCommunity IS NOT NULL
RETURN r.louvainCommunity as louvainCommunity
, count(*) as communityCount
ORDER BY communityCount DESC
LIMIT 10
```

Once we run this code, we can see that there are a couple of very large communities where many of the recipes are quite similar. Based on our exploratory analysis of the cornbread recipes in previous chapters, this is intuitive. Many of the recipes are duplicative with very similar ingredients. However, now that we have run community detection, new patterns have begun to emerge:

louvainCommunity	communityCount
542	2388
8535	2117
4205	766
2647	479
6906	359
7403	52
21	22
5750	6
5693	4
267	3

Figure 8.3: *Top 10 largest communities of the cornbread recipes*

For example, we can see that community #5750 contains only six recipes. This could be a good example for us to explore visually to better understand why this group was parsed from the largest communities with over 2000 recipes each:

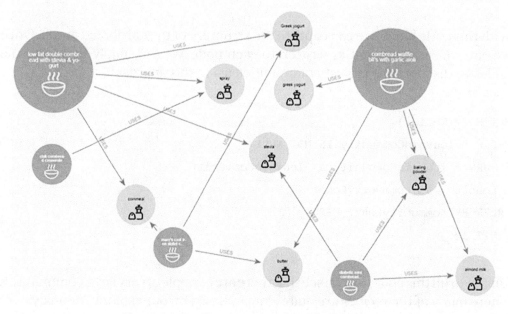

Figure 8.4: *Small community of cornbread recipes*

While some of the recipes and ingredients were removed from the image to enable it to fit on the page, we can see ingredients like "**greek yogurt**" and "**almond milk**" are ingredients used in this small community of cornbread recipes. These relatively unique ingredients explain why this community was broken apart from the larger network of cornbread recipes. These recipes use typical ingredients such as butter and salt, but their uniqueness helps separate these recipes from the rest.

Similarity

Similarity algorithms are designed to quantify the likeness or resemblance between nodes in a graph. These algorithms compare features of the graph, such as age or location between user nodes. The core idea is to determine how closely related the two nodes are to one another.

In the previous chapter, we have covered cosine similarity between node embeddings. Cosine similarity is a powerful, commonly used algorithm in the field of text analysis and **natural language processing (NLP)** because it measures the similarity between two vectors in a multi-dimensional space.

The different similarity algorithms provide advantages in different types of data and applications. In the next section, we will explore the Jaccard Similarity algorithm.

Jaccard Similarity Index

In this section, we will look into the Jaccard Similarity Index which is a commonly used method for quantifying the similarity between two sets. This approach will be particularly useful in scenarios where relationships between nodes define a node's membership, such as determining the similarity between recipes based on their shared ingredients.

The algorithm measures the intersection between two nodes and then divides by the size of the union of the sets. In the following example, we see two recipes "**Southern Cornbread**" and "**Vegan Cornbread**" and we want to measure the similarity between the two recipes based on their ingredients.

- Southern Cornbread = {cornmeal, flour, buttermilk, eggs, and butter}
- Vegan Cornbread = {cornmeal, flour, almond milk and, flaxseeds}

To compute the Jaccard Similarity Index, we first calculate the intersection (or common ingredients) which in this case is 2. Next, we divide by the union (all the ingredients) which in this case is 7. Therefore, the similarity index calculated by this algorithm is 2/7 or 28.5%.

Next, let's explore this algorithm implementation in Neo4j. We will use the same graph projection as before to project the cornbread recipes into an in-memory representation of the graph. We will then run the following code to stream the top 10 most similar recipes:

```
CALL gds.nodeSimilarity.stream('ingredients')
YIELD node1, node2, similarity
WITH gds.util.asNode(node1).Recipe_Title AS Recipe_Title1,
       gds.util.asNode(node2).Recipe_Title AS Recipe_Title2,
       similarity
WHERE Recipe_Title1 IS NOT NULL
RETURN *
ORDER BY similarity DESC
LIMIT 10;
```

In this example, we use the stream functionality to return the results of the query rather than write the results back to the database itself. When we run this query, the results look like this:

Recipe_Title1	Recipe_Title2	similarity
african-american cornbread	basic cornbread	1.0
african-american cornbread	yellow cornbread	1.0
"tot's" cornbread	cornbread from the south(johnnycake)	1.0
1st place state fair cornbread	buttery cornbread	1.0
(perfect) cornbread	perfect cornbread	1.0
african-american cornbread	cornbread	1.0
"mama's" cornbread	buttermilk cornbread	1.0
"cream of wheat" cornbread	tenth cloud cornbread(for those who cannot eat cornbread.)	1.0
"cream of wheat" cornbread	cornbread	1.0
alber's cornbread	cornbread	1.0

Figure 8.5: Similar cornbread recipes

These results indicate that all the recipes shown here share the same ingredients and are, therefore, quite similar. This approach can be helpful in deconflicting or resolving entities in your data where there are multiple duplicate nodes. If there are duplicate nodes as defined by similar community composition, then the Jaccard Similarity Index will quantify the similarity and allow you to deduplicate the data.

We can use this Cypher query to return a visual representation of all the shared ingredients between these two recipes to verify they do, in fact, share the same ingredients:

```
```

```
MATCH (r:Recipe)-[u:USES]->(i:Ingredient)
WHERE r.Recipe_Title IN ['african-american cornbread','basic cornbread']
    AND r.Recipe_ID IN [156423,1065844]
RETURN *
```

```
```

As we can see from the resulting image, all of the ingredients are shared between the two recipes:

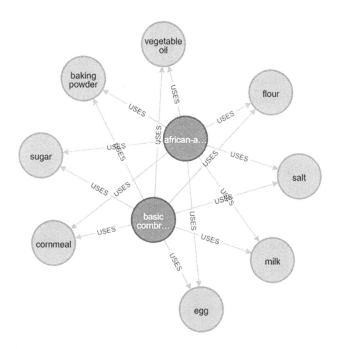

Figure 8.6: *Identical ingredients between recipes*

In conclusion, the Jaccard Similarity Index is a helpful, straightforward algorithm for comparing the intersection of sets between nodes to measure the similarity based on shared membership. However, this algorithm can be sensitive to size variations. In cases where the recipes significantly differ in the number of ingredients, for example, this could affect the similarity index. The simplicity and interpretability of this algorithm make it a popular choice for exploratory data analysis and similarity comparisons.

Link Prediction

Link prediction is a powerful approach to understanding potential connections within complex networks. In this section, we will showcase the popular algorithm Adamic-Adar Index. This technique goes beyond simply counting the number of connections shared between neighbors. Instead, it recognizes the significance of rare connections and weights these more heavily in the link prediction algorithm. For instance, in the case of the recipes and ingredients dataset, if two recipes share a unique spice, then this shared ingredient would be given a higher weight by the Adamic-Adar Index compared to the weight given to common ingredients such as milk or salt.

Link prediction can be a powerful tool across many domains, including social network analysis, recommendation systems, or e-commerce. In social networks, link prediction can help suggest new friends or connections by examining current connections and relationships of those connections to other individuals. In healthcare and drug discovery, link prediction can identify potential connections between drugs and diseases, helping pave the way to more effective treatments.

Adamic-Adar Index

The Adamic-Adar Index is a crucial aspect of graph data science, as it is known for its ability to identify potential connections within a network by emphasizing the importance of less common links. Conceptually, it is rooted in the idea that not all shared connections between nodes in a network are equally significant. If there are rare or uncommon connections, then these are weighted more heavily.

We can now apply this algorithm to the recipe dataset. The discovery of new and exciting recipes depends on the complex relationships between multiple ingredients. Using the Adamic-Adar Index, we can explore relationships between existing recipes to look for combinations of ingredients that may be novel and innovative.

To begin, we can use two of the cornbread recipes previously determined to be similar and calculate the Jaccard Similarity Index and Adamic-Adar Index between these two recipes:

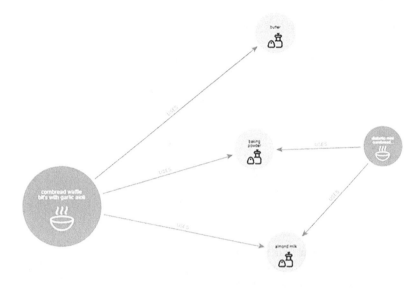

Figure 8.7: *Similar cornbread recipes*

In this figure, we can see the two recipes share two ingredients. The almond milk is a relatively unique ingredient in cornbread recipes. Therefore, we should expect these two recipes to have a higher similarity compared to other cornbread recipes.

When we run the following cypher query, we need to specify our anchor node, which, in this case, is the "cornbread waffle blt's with garlic aioli", as well as the search group to limit the amount of link prediction calculations required by the database. We will use the **louvaincommunity** ID to assist with limiting the search space:

```
```
MATCH (p1:Recipe)
 MATCH (p2:Recipe)
 WHERE p1.Recipe_ID = 1278977
    AND p2.louvainCommunity = 5750
 RETURN p1.Recipe_Title as Recipe_Title1
```
```

```
, p2.Recipe_Title as Recipe_Title2
, ROUND(gds.alpha.linkprediction.adamicAdar(p1, p2, {relationshipQuery:
'USES'}),3) AS score
ORDER BY score DESC
LIMIT 3
```

After executing the Adamic-Adar Index, we can see that the highest recommended recipe to our anchor recipe is indeed the "diabetic mini cornbread muffins."

Recipe_Title1	Recipe_Title2	score
cornbread waffle blt's with garlic aioli	diabetic mini cornbread muffins	0.326
cornbread waffle blt's with garlic aioli	mary's cast iron skillet cornbread	0.157
cornbread waffle blt's with garlic aioli	low fat double cornbread with stevia & yogurt	0.156

Figure 8.8: Link prediction results to anchor node

This approach to recommending similar nodes to the anchor node is a highly valuable technique. Not only are we able to navigate complex networks to parse the connections to our anchor node, but we are also able to automatically weight the connections based on relative frequency, which can boost the effectiveness of our analytics dramatically.

Network Embeddings and Graph Neural Network

Network embeddings and **graph neural networks (GNNs)** represent the cutting edge where artificial intelligence intersects with network science. This section dives into these advanced techniques, exploring the capabilities and applications of the algorithms to extract deep insights from graph-structured data.

The purpose of embedding graph structures is to preserve the structure of the graph while transforming the graph into a vector, computer-readable representation. This transformation facilitates many forms of analysis, including node classification and link prediction, as well as clustering and visualization.

GraphSAGE

GraphSAGE (Graph Sample and AggregatE) introduces a novel approach to GNNs by generating embeddings by sampling and aggregating features from a node's local neighborhood. GraphSAGE supports predictions on unseen data and is very scalable due to its sampling of a fixed number of neighbors for each node.

GraphSAGE can be useful in recommendation systems, node classification, link prediction, fraud detection, drug discovery, and more. In the following example, we will use the recipes dataset to demonstrate how GraphSAGE can be leveraged to embed ingredients and recipes into a vector space and use the embeddings to assess similarities and differences between recipes based on their ingredient composition.

We will first create a graph projection of all the nodes and recipes related to cornbread recipes.

```
```
MATCH (source:Recipe)-[:USES]->(target:Ingredient)
WHERE source.Recipe_Title CONTAINS 'cornbread'
    AND source.pageRank IS NOT NULL
    AND target.pageRank IS NOT NULL
WITH gds.graph.project(
  'ingredients',
  source,
  target,
  {
    sourceNodeProperties: source { pageRank: coalesce(source.pageRank,
0.001)},
    targetNodeProperties: target { pageRank: coalesce(target.pageRank,
0.001)}
  },
  {undirectedRelationshipTypes: ['*']}
) as g
RETURN
  g.graphName AS graph, g.nodeCount AS nodes, g.relationshipCount AS
rels
```
```

In this code, we specify that the source and target nodes must contain the property "pageRank" because the GraphSAGE algorithm in Neo4j requires a node property as an input.

Next, we will train the GraphSAGE algorithm to learn the structure of the projected graph. We will provide the `featureProperties`, the aggregator we wish to use, the number of iterations – or epochs – that we want the algorithm to loop through, and the searchDepth for the sampling of neighboring nodes required by the algorithm:

```
```

```
CALL gds.beta.graphSage.train(
  'ingredients',
  {
    modelName: 'graphSageModel',
    featureProperties: ['pageRank'],
    aggregator: 'mean',
    epochs: 5,
    searchDepth: 5
  }
)
YIELD modelInfo
RETURN modelInfo
```

```
```

Once we execute this code, we will see model statistics and metrics that reference the losses in each epoch iteration, as well as whether or not the model converges within the number of epochs provided.

Now that the GraphSAGE model has been created, we could take our analysis in multiple directions, including recommendation systems, node classification, link prediction, or visualization of the high dimensional space. For now, we will focus on visually representing the data.

For this exercise, we will use the algorithm UMAP, which helps visualize complex, high-dimensional data such as embeddings generated by GraphSAGE. In the following code, we use UMAP to reduce the multi-dimensional representation of recipes and ingredients and reduce them to a 2D space:

```
```

```python
import umap
import numpy as np
import pandas as pd
```

```
import plotly.express as px
from sklearn.cluster import KMeans


embeddings = np.array(df['embedding'].tolist())


reducer = umap.UMAP(n_neighbors=15,  # Try different values for n_neighbors
                    min_dist=0.1,    # Try different values for min_dist
                    random_state=42)
umap_embeddings = reducer.fit_transform(embeddings)


n_clusters = 10
kmeans = KMeans(n_clusters=n_clusters, random_state=42)
cluster_labels = kmeans.fit_predict(umap_embeddings)


umap_df = pd.DataFrame(umap_embeddings, columns=['x', 'y'])
umap_df['cluster'] = cluster_labels  # Add cluster labels to the DataFrame


# Plot using Plotly with cluster colors
fig = px.scatter(umap_df, x='x', y='y', color='cluster', title='2D UMAP
visualization of Recipe Embeddings with K-Means Clusters')
fig.update_traces(marker=dict(size=5))
fig.show()
```

In this code, the 'n_neighbors' in UMAP shapes how UMAP balances the local versus global structure, enabling the algorithm to capture the broader context of the network embedding. Similarly, the 'min_dist' parameter determines how tightly or loosely the points are grouped together in the reduced space. These parameters help dictate the granularity and separation of the data clusters.

Also, we use the K-Means clustering algorithm on the reduced embedding to represent collections of recipes that are similar to one another in the high-dimensional space of their GraphSAGE embeddings but can now be represented in 2D.

The Plotly visualization library adds depth to our data analysis by not only allowing us to visually explore the data but also zoom in and hover over data points on the scatter plot, which provides an additional, powerful capability to the visualization. The following image represents the reduced dimensions of the recipe embeddings using the UMAP algorithm.

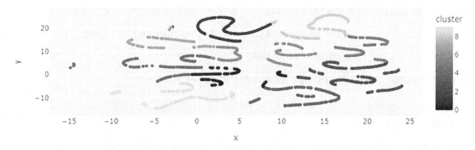

Figure 8.9: *Reduced dimensions of recipe embeddings with UMAP*

In this image, we can see all the cornbread recipes initially created in a high-dimensional space by the GraphSAGE algorithm and then reduced to a 2D representation by the UMAP algorithm. Finally, we use the K-Means algorithm to add a third dimension to the visualization to represent the cluster ID for each recipe and ingredient.

Conclusion

This chapter illustrated the importance of graph algorithms in interpreting and engaging with interconnected data. We explored the core areas of centrality, community detection, similarity, link prediction, and network embeddings. Each algorithm offers unique, actionable insights into interconnected data.

The Neo4j database offers these algorithms from within the database, making it a powerful tool for graph data science. The in-database analytics simplifies the data pipeline for data engineers and data scientists, ultimately leading to insights and action more quickly and effectively for end stakeholders.

While we only scratched the surface of graph algorithms in this chapter, we covered many of the foundational principles with the intent of opening the doors of your imagination to explore what other algorithms may be applicable to your specific use case. The power of graph data science lies in the ability to reveal huddle patterns in connected data which empower innovation and discovery. In the next two chapters, we will implement a few of these algorithms to apply to typical, real-world data science use cases.

Points to Remember

- **Graph Algorithms are Essential for Complex Network Analysis:** They play a crucial role in interpreting interconnected data structures. Graph algorithms help in navigating and understanding the web of interconnected data, revealing hidden patterns and relationships.

- **Types of Graph Algorithms Covered:**

  o **Centrality:** Identifies the most influential nodes within a network.

  o **Community Detection:** Discovers groups or clusters of nodes, highlighting the modular structure of the network.

  o **Similarity:** Measures the likeness or structural equivalence between nodes.

  o **Link Prediction**: Predicts the likelihood of the formation of a connection between two nodes.

- **Network Embeddings and Graph Neural Networks:** Utilizes advanced machine learning techniques to represent graph structures for deeper analysis.

Recommendation Engines Using Embeddings

Introduction

A recommendation engine is a tool designed to predict or present items most likely to be of interest to a user. The importance of the recommendations lies in the unique personalization of the user and user engagement in order to best assist with the users' decision-making process. If you think about popular streaming services such as Amazon or Netflix, these use recommendation engines to assist you with choosing the best movie based on your previous experiences.

Recommendation engines can be categorized into three categories:

- **Content-Based Filtering**: This approach aims to recommend content based on what the user has liked in the past. In the example of movie recommendations, this would involve suggesting movies similar to those the user has watched in the past.

- **Collaborative Filtering**: This method looks at similar users to guide recommendations for the current user. The idea behind this is that similar users will agree in the future about item preferences.

- **Hybrid Systems**: This combines both content-based and collaborative filtering to mitigate the limitations of each approach and often provide a more comprehensive recommendation.

Knowledge graphs enhance recommendation engines because of their inherent structure. The mapping of nodes by relationships is well-suited for enriched contextual analysis, scalability, and flexibility, as well as real-time recommendations. Finally, the knowledge graph structure caters well to graph-based algorithms like link prediction, which improves the overall accuracy of recommendations.

Structure

In this chapter, we will cover the following topics:

- Loading the Patent Database Dump into Neo4j Desktop
- Recommendation Engine Using the Retrieval-Augmented Generation (RAG) Approach
- Recommendation Engine Leveraging the RetrievalQA Approach

Patent Recommendations

To illustrate the concepts of recommendation engines, we will utilize the patent database. Patents are critical for innovation and research. They help provide legal protection for inventors and companies as they research and develop new innovations. Patents also serve as a valuable source of information providing insights into the latest advancements.

Patents are highly technical documents often written by lawyers and can often be complex. In addition to the complexity of reading the documents, the analysis of patents can be hindered by the sheer volume of information and the ambiguity of overlapping contexts between patents.

The **Retrieval-Augmented Generation (RAG)** process is an ideal methodology to use for this complex and rich data source. RAG can be used to retrieve relevant patents, enrich the patents with additional information, and ultimately generate insights and recommendations for the user. RAG in patent analysis can overcome some of the typical challenges faced in patent research.

Loading Patent Data

To begin, we need to load the Patent database to our Neo4j Desktop database. We can create a new database, called Patents, and utilize the latest version of Neo4j to ensure we have vector storage installed:

Name

≋ Patents

Password

🔒 password

Version

5.16.0 (latest)　　　　　　　　　　　　　　　　　　　　　▾

✕ Cancel　　✓ Create

Figure 9.1: *Create new Patents database*

We are going to import the Patents database dump from the accompanying file for this chapter. Once your new Patents database has been created from the previous step, navigate to **Open Folder** in Neo4j Desktop and then click **DBMS**:

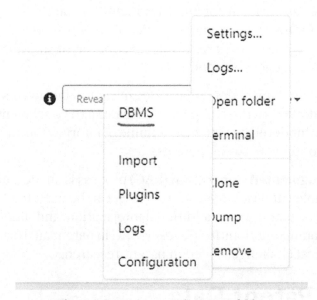

Settings...

Logs...

ℹ Revea　　　　　　　　)pen folder ▾

DBMS　　　　　　　erminal

Import　　　　　　　　lone

Plugins　　　　　　　)ump

Logs　　　　　　　　　emove

Configuration

Figure 9.2: *Navigate to the DBMS folder*

Once you click DBMS, a file explorer will appear. This will provide the path needed to import the Patent database dump file. The file explorer path should appear something like this:

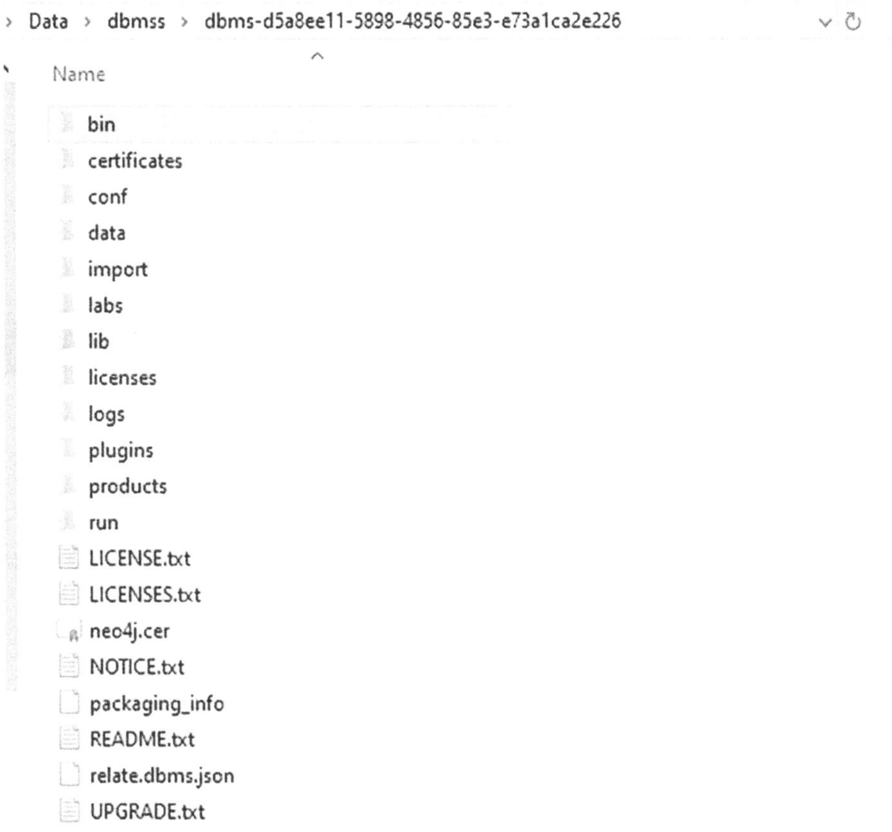
› Data › dbmss › dbms-d5a8ee11-5898-4856-85e3-e73a1ca2e226
Name
bin
certificates
conf
data
import
labs
lib
licenses
logs
plugins
products
run
LICENSE.txt
LICENSES.txt
neo4j.cer
NOTICE.txt
packaging_info
README.txt
relate.dbms.json
UPGRADE.txt

Figure 9.3: *Path to the bin folder*

The file explorer will show you the path to the bin folder. Once you have the bin folder, navigate to the bin directory and then copy the path to the bin folder. For example, here is the file path provided to a Windows user:

```
C:\Users\TimEa\AppData\Local\Neo4j\Relate\Data\dbmss\dbms-d5a8ee11-5898-4856-85e3-e73a1ca2e226\bin
```

Next, you will need to open a command prompt and add '**cd**' to the beginning of the path to your Neo4j Database bin directory from the previous step. Once you click Enter, you will now access the bin directory of your new Neo4j database:

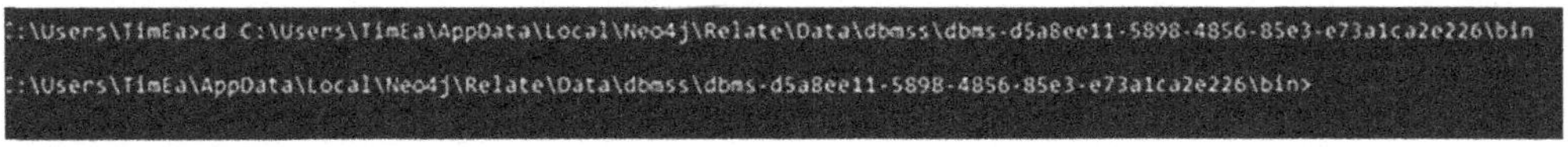
:\Users\TimEa>cd C:\Users\TimEa\AppData\Local\Neo4j\Relate\Data\dbmss\dbms-d5a8ee11-5898-4856-85e3-e73a1ca2e226\bin
:\Users\TimEa\AppData\Local\Neo4j\Relate\Data\dbmss\dbms-d5a8ee11-5898-4856-85e3-e73a1ca2e226\bin>

Figure 9.4: *Access to the bin directory of your new Patent database*

Once you see that you are in the bin directory of your new Patent database, as shown above, run the following command to load the dump file from your saved location into the Neo4j Database bin folder. The file needs to be named "neo4j. dump" for this command to function properly:

```
```
neo4j-admin database load neo4j --from-path=C:\Users\TimEa\Downloads\
Patents patents --overwrite-destination=true
```
```

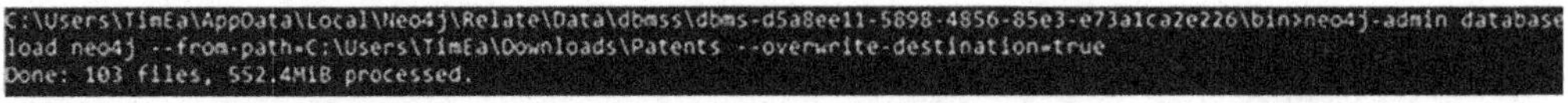

Figure 9.5: *Success message after loading the Patent database dump*

Congratulations, you have successfully loaded the database dump of patent data into your new Patent database! This will enable you to run GDS and APOC functions that enable us to run graph data science functions directly on our graph data for free. Go ahead and install these plugins, if you have not already, so that you can use these functions later.

RAG Retrieval for Patents

As we mentioned at the beginning of this chapter, recommendation engines can involve multiple approaches and methodologies. For this example, we will focus on patent retrieval using content-based filtering with text analysis. This method involves analyzing the text to extract meaning and provide relevant and precise recommendations. This way, we can accurately match patents with user interests and enhance the search engine with precise recommendations.

The first step in running a **Retrieval-Augmented Generation (RAG)** process with Neo4j as the backend database is to connect to the vector index. The name of the vector index in our Patent database is 'embeddingsindex.' To proceed with this example, you will need to obtain an OpenAI key:

```
```
embedding_provider = OpenAIEmbeddings()

patent_abstract_vector = Neo4jVector.from_existing_index(
    embedding_provider,
    url=uri,
    username=user,
```
```

```
    password=pw,

    index_name="embeddingsindex",

    embedding_node_property="embedding",

    text_node_property="abstract",

)
```
```

Once we connect to the vector index, we can use the earlier `patent_abstract_vector` variable to run a similarity search of a new description or persona. For example, we can run the following code to find the single most similar patent to our given description:

```

```
r = patent_abstract_vector.similarity_search("A system for removing an
occlusive clot from a blood vessel.", k=1)

print(r)
```
```

We set k=1 in this example to return the single closest description to our given persona. The result is a patent titled '**CLOT RETRIEVAL SYSTEM FOR REMOVING OCCLUSIVE CLOT FROM A BLOOD VESSEL**' and, unsurprisingly, the abstract description of the patent matches the persona nicely: "*A system for removing an occlusive clot from a blood vessel comprises a catheter and an apparatus for generating a pulsatile vacuum force to pulse the pressure gradient at a distal end of the catheter. The pulse generator may be integral with or separate from the vacuum pump. The pulse generator may be applied to a flexible tubing between the vacuum pump and the proximal end of the catheter.*"

We can use this same methodology to filter false positives from a list of potential matches. For example, imagine you search your database for any patent related to **virtual reality (VR)** capabilities. Unfortunately, you may return thousands of potential hits. Many of these responses may be incorrect and inaccurate. We can use the RAG methodology to rank the most similar responses to our persona description and then set a cutoff to filter out many of the false positives.

In this following code, we now return the first 1000 patents that match our description. As you will see next, many of the 1000 responses toward the bottom of the list are false positives:
```

```
```
r = patent_abstract_vector.similarity_search("An immersive VR system
designed for education.", k=1000)

pd.set_option('display.max_columns', None)
pd.set_option('display.width', None)
pd.set_option('display.max_colwidth', None)

data_list = []
for document in r:
    page_content = document.page_content
    title = document.metadata['title']
    data_list.append({'Title': title})

df = pd.DataFrame(data_list)
display(df)
```
```

After running this code, we will notice that rows 0-4 closely match the persona provided for virtual reality. On the other hand, rows 995-999 may reference virtual reality in their personas, but it's evident that virtual reality is not the primary focus or purpose of those patents:

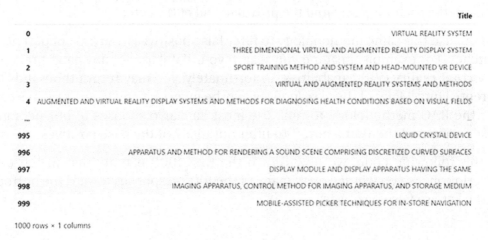

	Title
0	VIRTUAL REALITY SYSTEM
1	THREE DIMENSIONAL VIRTUAL AND AUGMENTED REALITY DISPLAY SYSTEM
2	SPORT TRAINING METHOD AND SYSTEM AND HEAD-MOUNTED VR DEVICE
3	VIRTUAL AND AUGMENTED REALITY SYSTEMS AND METHODS
4	AUGMENTED AND VIRTUAL REALITY DISPLAY SYSTEMS AND METHODS FOR DIAGNOSING HEALTH CONDITIONS BASED ON VISUAL FIELDS
...	...
995	LIQUID CRYSTAL DEVICE
996	APPARATUS AND METHOD FOR RENDERING A SOUND SCENE COMPRISING DISCRETIZED CURVED SURFACES
997	DISPLAY MODULE AND DISPLAY APPARATUS HAVING THE SAME
998	IMAGING APPARATUS, CONTROL METHOD FOR IMAGING APPARATUS, AND STORAGE MEDIUM
999	MOBILE-ASSISTED PICKER TECHNIQUES FOR IN-STORE NAVIGATION

1000 rows × 1 columns

Figure 9.6: *Virtual reality patent responses*

To summarize, RAG can be a terrific recommendation engine for text-based searches. In complex domains, such as patents, the RAG implementation is critical to maintaining the semantic essence of the text while sifting through false positive matches.

RetrievalQA Chains for Patents

Beyond the semantic similarity search offered by the RAG implementation, we can also run a **Retrieval Questions Answering** (`RetrievalQA`) chain query. This is used to combine LLM responses with external, proprietary databases. The Retrieval component queries an external data source or document collection – in this case, Neo4j. This information is then passed to an LLM to generate a more informed, accurate, and relevant response. This can be very useful in a Chatbot app where the information returned to the user needs to be up-to-date and relevant.

We can run the following code to provide a prompt to the LLM as well as request the LLM to query our Neo4j database:

```
```
retrievalQA = RetrievalQA.from_llm(
    llm=chat_llm,
    retriever=patent_abstract_vector.as_retriever(),
    verbose=True,
    return_source_documents=True
)

response = retrievalQA(f"""
You are a patent expert. You provide insights and recommendations on
patents based on their content, technology, and inventors.

I am researching wearable technology for health monitoring. Can you
recommend some patents that I should look into?
""")
```
```

When we run this **RetrievalQA** against our Neo4j database, we see the following response:

"Based on your interest in wearable technology for health monitoring, here are a few patents that you may find relevant:

1. US Patent No. 9,123,345: "Wearable Health Monitoring System"

2. US Patent No. 10,265,482: "Wearable Device for Physiological Monitoring"

3. US Patent No. 8,946,135: "Wearable Sensor System for Monitoring Vital Signs"

4. US Patent No. 10,617,492: "Wearable Device for Remote Health Monitoring"

5. US Patent No. 9,752,837: "Wearable Biometric Monitoring Device"

Please note that patent numbers and titles are provided for reference purposes, and you should conduct a thorough search and analysis to determine the specific patents that best suit your research needs.

This response from the LLM is powerful because it queries the information directly from our database and simultaneously enriches the query response using the power of the GPT model.

To summarize, `RetrievalQA` chains can also be a powerful tool to build your recommendation engines because they combine the power of LLMs with the proprietary data stored on your database.

Conclusion

In this chapter, we first reviewed the steps required to import the Neo4j database dump onto a Neo4j Desktop database. This is a critical step as it enables us to run GDS and APOC libraries to execute graph data science algorithms for free, which are required for our embedding similarity searches.

We also explored the innovative field of patent retrieval and recommendation by leveraging both the capabilities of **Retrieval-Augmented Generation (RAG)** and `RetrievalQA` chains. These advanced techniques can transform the landscape of patent analysis and search methodologies, offering more precise, relevant, and insightful recommendations.

The RAG methodology focuses on content-based filtering using text analysis, which enables nuanced retrieval of complex patent data. By connecting the vector index in Neo4j and utilizing similarity searches, we demonstrate how to enhance the precision of patent search engines.

We also covered the `RetrievalQA` chains, which integrate the responses of LLMs, such as GPT, with the data stored in our Neo4j database. This integration enables a sophisticated chatbot capable of providing up-to-date and relevant recommendations.

The implications of this technology are profound. They provide us with the unparalleled ability to sift through massive amounts of data and identify connections and insights that might have otherwise never been seen. For professionals in **intellectual property (IP)**, **research and development (R&D)**, or other cutting-edge fields, these tools can offer the means to stay ahead of the competition, innovate, and position yourself with a strategic advantage.

In the next chapter, we will discuss a common use case for graph data science: fraud detection. We will explore how connections between clients can indicate fraudulent behavior, as well as discuss methods for retrieving and exploring this information from the database.

Points to Remember

- Retrieval-Augmented Generation (RAG) uses content-based filtering to extract meaningful information from text.
- Neo4j is a terrific backend tool for RAG applications. Python allows us to easily interact with both OpenAI's GPT model as well as the stored embeddings in Neo4j.
- RAG methodologies provide similarity scores to help us sort and filter potential false positives from our initial result sets.
- `RetrievalQA` combines responses from large language models with data from Neo4j to provide timely and relevant recommendations.
- The combination of AI models and Neo4j enhances the ability to analyze and recommend result sets accurately and efficiently.

CHAPTER 10

Fraud Detection

Introduction

Digital transactions comprise billions of data points each day and require cutting-edge technology to combat the data challenges in the fraud landscape. Fraud schemes, such as identity theft, lead to significant economic losses as well as reputational risk for financial service companies.

Ultimately, fraud is an action of misrepresentation of facts for personal gain. It impacts many sectors such as finance, healthcare, online retail, and government services. With the rise of artificial intelligence, fraud schemes become increasingly more complicated to decipher and untangle. This requires a shift toward advanced analytical techniques, such as knowledge graphs, in order to analyze the interconnected relationships.

Understanding the different types of fraud is important for effective fraud detection. Here are some of the common terms and definitions used in fraud detection:

- **First-Party Fraud**: This occurs when an individual or entity misrepresents their own identity or provides false information for financial gain. Common examples include fabricating false information to obtain loans or credit or falsifying personal information to obtain benefits or services. In other words, this is the primary beneficiary of the financial deceit.

- **Second-Party Fraud**: This involves the complicit involvement of a second party within the fraud scheme. For example, an individual could willingly give personal information to another person who then uses it for fraudulent purposes.

- **Third-Party Fraud**: This is the most common type of fraud where an external individual or entity is stealing or using someone else's identity or information without their knowledge. This includes identity theft, account takeover, and credit card fraud.

Knowledge graphs offer a powerful tool in the fight against fraud by mapping complex relationships in vast datasets to pinpoint risk both algorithmically and visually. In this chapter, we will use Neo4j's graph data science library to detect patterns that are indicative of fraudulent activity and provide the foundational understanding of how knowledge graphs can help identify fraud in a new era of big data.

Structure

In this chapter, we will cover the following topics:

- Exploratory Analysis of Fraud Detection Dataset
- Connection Identifiers Commonly Used in Fraud Detection
- Data Engineering and Enriching the Fraud Dataset
- Graph Data Science for Fraud Detection

Exploratory Analysis of the Fraud Detection Dataset

We will use mock data in this chapter based on the Neo4j database dump available at: https://github.com/ava-orange-education/Graph-Data-Science-with-Python-and-Neo4j/tree/main/Chapter_10/Fraud_Detection. Neo4j has posted this dataset on their GitHub repository for training purposes. We will follow much of the same methodologies and guides that Neo4j outlined in their GitHub demo, presented in this chapter in a streamlined, easy-to-follow format.

To get started, we will first need to load the database dump file saved with the reference material for this chapter. To load the database dump file, follow the same steps as we walked through in the previous chapter.

Our first step of analysis will be to check the counts of nodes and relationships by type. With the following code, we can use the APOC library to concatenate the node label with the count by label:

```
CALL db.labels() YIELD label
    CALL apoc.cypher.run('MATCH (:`'+label+'`) RETURN count(*) as
count', {})
    YIELD value
```

```
    RETURN label as Label, value.count AS Count
    ORDER BY Count DESC
```

On running this Cypher query, we can see the following result:

Label	Count
Transaction	323489
CashIn	149037
CashOut	76023
Payment	74577
Transfer	19460
Debit	4392
Client	2433
SSN	2238
Phone	2234
Email	2229
Mule	433
Merchant	347
Bank	3

Figure 10.1: Count of node labels in fraud detection dataset

The transaction node is the most frequent node. The Client and SSN nodes are also very important nodes, as they help identify the source of potential fraud.

Next, we will want to understand the count of relationship types in the database. Similarly, we can use the APOC library to concatenate the types:

```
    CALL db.relationshipTypes() YIELD relationshipType as type
    CALL apoc.cypher.run('MATCH ()-[:`'+type+'`]->() RETURN count(*) as
count', {})
    YIELD value
    RETURN type AS Relationship, value.count AS Count
    ORDER BY Count DESC
```

On running this code, we can see the following results:

Relationship	Count
PERFORMED	323489
TO	323489
NEXT	321157
HAS_SSN	2433
HAS_EMAIL	2433
HAS_PHONE	2433
FIRST_TX	2332
LAST_TX	2332

Figure 10.2: *Count of relationship types in fraud detection dataset*

The PERFORMED relationship is the most common relationship, which represents the entity performing a transaction or action within the data.

The next step in our analysis is to create a relationship between clients who share the same attributes. In fraud detection, some of the attributes we could use to link clients together include:

- **Social Security Number (SSN)**: In the United States, the government issues a unique identification to each citizen called the SSN. If multiple clients are using the same SSN, this could be suspicious and may indicate identity theft.

- **Suspicious Activity Report (SAR)**: In the United States, financial institutions are required to file SARs on suspicious financial transactions. These can often reference multiple SSNs, which create connections between entities and can be used to link together fraud schemes.

- **Internet Protocol (IP) Address**: IP addresses identify the host or network and location of the network. Multiple clients sharing the same IP address could link together potential fraudsters.

- **Email**: Clients using the same email address could be potentially suspicious.

- **Phone**: Clients using the same phone number could be potentially suspicious.

- **Bank Accounts**: Shared bank accounts between different clients could be a red flag, especially if these accounts are used in suspicious transactions.

- **Employer**: Links can be established between clients based on shared employers.

- **Physical Address**: Shared residential or mailing addresses can link clients. Multiple clients linked to the same physical address or PO box could be potentially suspicious.

As you can imagine, many of these attributes can be used to link together clients and create a complex, tangled web of relationships between clients. The analysis of this web using a graph database like Neo4j can reveal hidden patterns that may not be apparent or obvious through traditional data analysis methods. In our mock data, we are limited to connections between clients based solely on:

1. Transaction behavior

2. SSNs

3. Phones

4. Emails

Our challenge for the remainder of this chapter will be to use these four connection criteria to dynamically map groups of customers. We will look to pinpoint potentially suspicious in the sections ahead that could be indicative of fraud.

Data Engineering

The first step towards stitching together potentially suspicious clients is to flag "Super Nodes" or nodes that have a high number of connections. Counting the number of relationships to each node serves two purposes:

- **Filter Criteria**: We can filter out false connections that could be data quality errors, which would result in false positive connections between clients. For example, if more than 100 clients say that their phone number is 999-999-9999, then we would want to have a property called 'node_degree' on the phone node to indicate that this phone number is potentially false and could be excluded from community detection.

- **Stand-Alone "Super Node" Analytics**: The degree of a node may enable a parallel analytics fraud project to dig into the underlying data to understand why "Super Nodes" exist in the first place. While the connections between clients may not be valid for community detection, there may be evidence of fraud based on a large number of connections.

We can run the following code to add an incoming as well as an outgoing degree for each node:

```
CALL apoc.periodic.iterate(
  'MATCH (n) RETURN n',
  'WITH n
  CALL {
      WITH n
      MATCH (n)-->()
      RETURN COUNT(*) AS out_degree
  }
  CALL {
      WITH n
      MATCH (n)<--()
      RETURN COUNT(*) AS in_degree
  }
  SET n.in_degree = in_degree, n.out_degree = out_degree
  RETURN n',
  {batchSize:1000}
)
```

Once we know the degree for each node, we can run a stand-alone "Super Node" analysis. For example, we can begin with the Email node to determine the most commonly used email addresses using the following cypher code:

```
MATCH (n:Email)
WITH n, n.in_degree + n.out_degree AS total_degree, labels(n) AS labels
ORDER BY total_degree DESC
RETURN n.email as email, labels, total_degree
LIMIT 10
```

This query will result in a list of the most commonly used email addresses with the highest count as 10:

email	labels	total_degree
kimberlyconley67@yahoo.com	[Email]	8
laylazimmerman09@mail.com	[Email]	6
sophiachan88@yahoo.com	[Email]	6
wood78@mail.com	[Email]	5
allison.anthony44@gmail.com	[Email]	5
bullock23@yahoo.com	[Email]	5
alyssa.clay89@yahoo.com	[Email]	5
spears63@mail.com	[Email]	5
ryan.powers25@gmail.com	[Email]	5
bennett21@yahoo.com	[Email]	5

Figure 10.3: *Degree of the Email nodes*

While this is mock data, we can easily imagine a real-world dataset with hundreds of clients using the same email address. Many times, an email could be fake or auto-generated such as "NONE@NA.com". These fake emails can be excluded from the analysis or used to fix data quality issues at the source.

Next, we will create a new relationship between customers called 'SHARED_ IDENTIFIER' when two customers share one or more of the aforementioned identifiers. To accomplish this, we can execute the following Cypher query:

```
MATCH (c1:Client)-[r:HAS_EMAIL|HAS_PHONE|HAS_SSN]->(n)<-
[r2:HAS_EMAIL|HAS_PHONE|HAS_SSN]-(c2:Client)
WHERE id(c1) < id(c2)
WITH c1, c2, count(*) as cnt,
    SUM(
        CASE WHEN type(r) = 'HAS_EMAIL' THEN 1
            WHEN type(r) = 'HAS_PHONE' THEN 1.5
            WHEN type(r) = 'HAS_SSN' THEN 5
            ELSE 0
        END
    ) AS weight
MERGE (c1)-[:SHARED_IDENTIFIERS {count: cnt, weight: weight}]->(c2);
```

In this command, we anchor between two clients (c1 and c2) and search for their common identifier that indirectly connects these two nodes. We search between Email, Phone, and SSN connections, as these attributes are currently available in our database. We also count the number of shared connections and add this as a property on the SHARED_IDENTIFERS relationship, which now directly maps the two clients. Furthermore, we can include business rules to help determine the weight or strength of connection between two clients. For example, if two clients share two of the same emails and four of the same phones, then the weight of connection on their SHARED_IDENTIFIERS relationship would be 8 (where 8 = 1.0 * 2 + 1.5 * 4). This weight will be useful when we run graph algorithms that can leverage weighted relationships in their calculations.

Graph Data Science for Fraud Detection

Once we have created a weighted link between clients sharing identifiers, the next step is to create an undirected graph of all these connections and pass the weight property into the graph projection as well:

```
CALL gds.graph.project('pg1',
    {
        Client: {
            label: 'Client'
        }
    },
    {
        SHARED_IDENTIFIERS:{
            type: 'SHARED_IDENTIFIERS',
            orientation: 'UNDIRECTED',
            properties: {
                count: {
                    property: 'weight'
                }
            }
        }
    }
) YIELD graphName,nodeCount,relationshipCount,projectMillis;
```

This code snippet is used to generate a graph projection, which effectively restructures the data from the knowledge graph into a format optimized for in-memory storage. This optimized format is particularly designed to facilitate the efficient execution of graph data science algorithms, enabling faster and more effective data processing and analysis.

Now that the data is in a projected graph in-memory, we can create communities of clients by running the Weakly Connected Components algorithm. This community detection algorithm assigns a unique ID to any nodes sharing a link between them. In very large datasets, this efficient algorithm can identify clients in groups of tens of thousands based on shared connections:

```
CALL gds.wcc.write('pg1', { writeProperty: 'WCC_ID' })
YIELD nodePropertiesWritten, componentCount;
```

Now that each customer has been assigned a unique ID for their community (called `WCC_ID`), we can visualize these communities (see *Figure 10.4*):

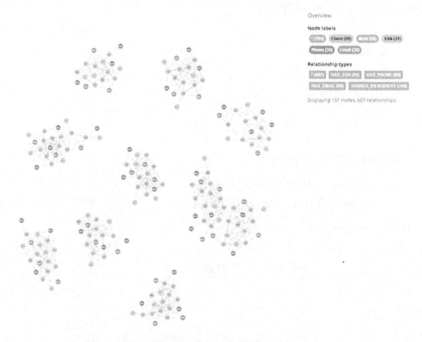

Figure 10.4: *Groups of potential fraud rings*

In *Figure 10.4*, we can see nine distinct groups of clients. Each group consists of clients who share identifiers with one another. For example, when we zoom in on one of these communities, we can see several clients linked to each other through various connections such as phone, email, and SSN:

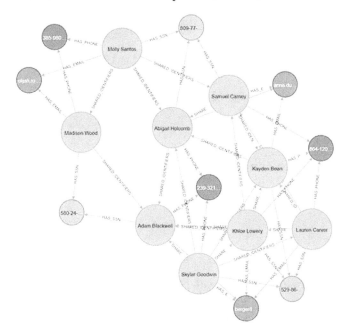

Figure 10.5: *Groups of potential fraud rings*

In the preceding figure, we can see nine clients in blue linked to one another through a combination of connections, including:

- 3 phone numbers
- 3 email addresses
- 3 SSNs

These communities are powerful in fraud detection because they link together entities that may be otherwise computationally inefficient or impossible to discover through traditional SQL and relational database approaches. As the size of the data grows, the need for a knowledge graph to stitch together disparate connections becomes increasingly necessary.

For example, in the preceding figure, we can see Lauren Carver is indirectly connected to Molly Santos because Lauren shares a phone with Samuel who then shares an SSN with Molly.

Neo4j also offers powerful path-finding algorithms, which can prove valuable in these situations. As you can imagine, these fraud networks can become quite large with sometimes thousands of clients connected to one another. You may find yourself in a situation where you know of one suspicious person and would like to find the shortest path from this person to someone else within the community. To accomplish this, we can use the appropriately named "shortest path" algorithm:

```
MATCH (start:Client {name: "Lauren Carver"}), (end:Client {name: "Molly
Santos"})
MATCH path = shortestPath((start)-[*]-(end))
RETURN path
```

On running this query, we can see the shortest path between Lauren and Molly is indeed through Samuel:

Figure 10.6: *Shortest path between Lauren and Molly*

The shortest path algorithm can be helpful in fraud detection for mapping linkages between potential fraudsters within the same weakly connected component communities. It can also be a helpful algorithm to use in industries like Logistics when one needs to analyze the supply chain and the shortest path between two points.

In large communities, it is helpful to use node centrality measures to identify which nodes are most important or influential within the network. One centrality measure that is commonly used in fraud detection is the Eigenvector Centrality algorithm. This approach helps to uncover potentially fraudulent nodes that are central in a network of complex relationships. Eigenvector Centrality provides a deeper insight into the network structure, highlighting nodes that are central to the connectivity and flow within the community.

```
CALL gds.eigenvector.write('pg1', {
  maxIterations: 20,
  writeProperty: 'eigenvectorCentrality'
})
YIELD nodePropertiesWritten, ranIterations
```

When we run this code on our graph projection, we now have the node centrality score assigned to each node. With this in mind, we can run the following code to determine the communities with the clients with the highest connectivity scores:

```
MATCH (c:Client)
WITH c.WCC_ID as WCC_ID, max(c.eigenvectorCentrality) as eigenvectorCen-
trality
RETURN WCC_ID, ROUND(eigenvectorCentrality,2) as eigenvectorCentrality
ORDER BY eigenvectorCentrality DESC
LIMIT 5
```

On executing this Cypher query, we can see community 1865 has the client with the highest connectivity score. The following image shows Lauren Hayden as the client with the highest centrality score of 0.32 within this community:

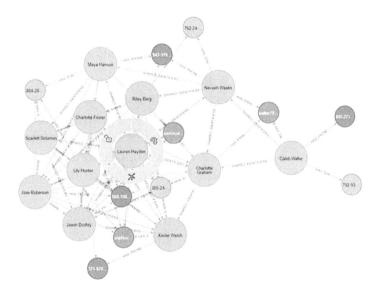

Figure 10.7: *Node centrality using Eigenvector Algorithm*

While Lauren Hayden is highly connected within this community, resulting in a high Eigenvector score, this community remains relatively small. In large-scale fraud detection, the node centrality algorithms are extremely important because they help pinpoint the primary bad actor within the network.

In fraud detection, it is important to identify the initial lead subject to assist investigation teams. Large-scale criminal networks are cumbersome and unwieldy. Given the sensitive and often confidential nature of the data involved, investigators are tasked with meticulously sifting through the information. This careful analysis is critical as it ensures the accuracy of the findings and also maintains the integrity of the investigation, as well as providing protection to the privacy of individuals. Therefore, implementing precise and efficient data analysis methods, like those mentioned here, becomes invaluable in isolating the key subjects and unraveling the broader network of fraudulent activities.

Conclusion

In this chapter, we explored the intricacies of fraud detection and utilized the power of Neo4j to unravel the web of connections. Utilizing mock data, we emulated real-world scenarios to illustrate how graph technology can unmask fraud.

Initially, we loaded the database using a database dump and explored the relationships between clients based on transactions and shared indicators such as phone, email, and SSN. We also took the important step of creating direct connections between clients based on these shared connections.

An important aspect of working with large networks with potentially falsified data is to examine and flag the presence of "*Super Nodes.*" Super-nodes can act as the starting point for fraud analysis as these are straightforward counts of the largest number of connections within the network. However, these can also prove to be problematic if these are not "real connections" between clients (for example, "NA@NONE.com" email address). We explore techniques to flag and remove these connections from our analysis.

Additionally, we implemented graph algorithms such as community detection, node centrality, and shortest path techniques to illustrate how we can use the power of knowledge graphs to make the analysis of large networks more manageable and efficient. These techniques reveal central figures in potential fraud rings, which offer valuable insights in fraud detection.

In conclusion, this chapter demonstrated the efficacy of Neo4j in the unraveling of complex fraud rings. Through a detailed approach, we took mock data and approached a real-world fraud detection challenge and highlighted the importance of graph databases in modern data analytics and criminal investigations.

In the next chapter, we will wrap up our discussion of graph data science and explore what these analytics may look like in the future. This technology continues to expand and change each day, and there is immense opportunity for the future.

Multiple Choice Questions

1. Identifying Connections: In the context of fraud detection using Neo4j, which of the following attributes is NOT typically used to link clients together?

   A. Social Security Number (SSN)

   B. Favorite Color

   C. Email Address

   D. IP Address

2. Understanding Graph Algorithms: Which graph algorithm is commonly used in Neo4j for community detection in fraud analysis?

   A. Shortest Path

   B. PageRank

   C. Weakly Connected Components

   D. A* Algorithm

3. Exploring Node Relationships: In our Neo4j fraud detection dataset, what does a 'SHARED_IDENTIFIERS' relationship between two Client nodes indicate?

   A. Both clients have the same bank account

   B. Both clients are employed at the same company

   C. Both clients share common identifiers like SSN, Email, or Phone

   D. Both clients have conducted transactions at the same time

Answers

1. B

2. C

3. C

The Future of Graph Data Science

Introduction

Let us now reflect on our journey through graph data science thus far. We have explored how this method of storing data in the form of nodes and relationships unlocks hidden potential in data to uncover new patterns and new insights. We showcased how we can unravel a complex web of connections to highlight the key influencers within a network, how to create communities of customers, and how to merge the power of embeddings with the explainable nature of knowledge graphs.

Just as our brains think of people and interactions as networks, we should also store our data in a format that represents the true nature of data. This way, we understand the linkages and interactions. Storing our data in this format also benefits us because we can run algorithms designed specifically for graph data structures, such as node centrality, community detection, and graph neural network algorithms.

In this chapter, we seek to leverage the knowledge of what we have learned to formulate a reasonable outlook into the future of this technology. While we have thoroughly explored the current state of graph data science and its capabilities, we believe that this field is growing rapidly. Let us explore areas where graph data science may continue to expand in the future.

The Evolution of Graph Technology

The landscape of "*Big Data*" is undergoing a major shift driven by the exponential increase in the volume and complexity of data. The challenge is no longer in simply handling vast quantities of data but also in extracting valuable information and actionable insights from it. This need for deeper understanding is propelling the evolution of graph technology.

Graph data science has emerged as an essential tool for this new era of data transformation and knowledge extraction. Its libraries are expanding rapidly, and new algorithms are being designed to tackle these increasingly complex data challenges. These new algorithms represent a paradigm shift in data analysis because they represent more than rows and columns, offering a holistic approach to solving complex, interconnected problems.

This paradigm shift to unlock new dimensions of knowledge connects directly to the advancements in **Large Language Models (LLMs)**. There is a timely and necessary integration opportunity in storing LLM embeddings within knowledge graphs. This integration with models like GPT offers a revolutionary opportunity to understand the contextual relationships between both structured and unstructured data in a manner that was previously not possible. These synergies offer a new frontier in data science.

As we continue to witness the growth of both the size and complexity of data, the importance of knowledge graphs in conjunction with LLMs will only become more pronounced. In doing so, we make significant progress in not only managing our data but also in understanding it and harnessing its full potential.

Key Takeaways from the Book

This book serves as a comprehensive guide to the interesting realm of graph data science, offering a blend of foundational theory with hands-on applications. It is designed to assist those venturing into this field as well as seasoned practitioners looking to deepen their understanding and skills in this new era of LLMs and knowledge graphs.

We started by reviewing the fundamentals of graph data science. We spoke about the distinction between nodes, relationships, and properties, which serve as the foundational building blocks of our knowledge graph analysis. We also walked through data modeling and data import, which serve as the beginnings for the advanced topics.

A significant highlight of the book is the integration between Python and Neo4j, which offers the versatility of the Python programming language as well as the toolkits and processing capabilities of the Neo4j database, providing powerful in-database analytics. We discussed how Python can enhance the functionality of Neo4j and, combined, can enable data scientists to quickly incorporate the power of graph data science into their production pipelines.

Data modeling and import techniques are critical to graph data science projects. The size and complexity of datasets require techniques, including importing data from common sources such as CSV, JSON, and APIs. We also covered how to load database dump files into both Neo4j Desktop as well as the Aura database. Finally, we discussed the Admin import, which is the fastest way to import new data into Neo4j.

We also dove into mastering the Cypher query language. Cypher is used in several graph database technologies and was originally created by Neo4j. We explored the basic CRUD (Create, Read, Update, Delete) commands as well as more advanced pattern matching, aggregations, and subqueries. The book also covered the Profile and Explain commands to tune the performance of Cypher queries.

Regarding visualization for graph data science, we discussed the pivotal role of visually representing the connections between graph data. Often, analysts will use spreadsheets to interpret connections between text and numbers. Visualizations with tools like Neo4j Bloom transform the data into a format that is more accessible, intuitive, and actionable. In addition to Bloom, we examined third-party tools and Python libraries that offer extended functionality and customization options.

By integrating OpenAI's ChatGPT into our workstream, we demonstrated the new possibilities available to our data pipelines. We illustrated how to enhance graph data with AI insights through added text content and updating our knowledge graph accordingly. We also showcased how we can convert this text into embeddings, or computer-readable vectors that maintain the contextual information of the text, within Neo4j directly. The ability to store embeddings directly within Neo4j is powerful because we only need to embed the text once, store the embeddings in the database, and then pull an immense amount of information from these embeddings. We showcased how we can run similarity searches between texts by comparing the distances between the two text's embeddings. This approach enables us to update the knowledge graph with a new relationship linking the two similar texts to one another based on the distance between their embeddings.

The concept of **retrieval-augmented generation (RAG)** represents a leap forward in efficient and accurate retrieval of text information by leveraging the embedding output from LLMs like GPT-4. Vector indexing is crucial in large-scale applications where quick access to information is critical. Neo4j supports vector indexing and enables us to build RAG applications with Neo4j as the backend database.

We also covered a few of the many graph data science algorithms available in Neo4j, which helps us in topics of node importance, community detection, path finding, and graph embeddings. Several of these algorithms were illustrated using practical examples, including the recipe dataset. Numerous algorithms can be discovered by referencing the Neo4j documentation.

Personal recommendations are prolific in current data products offered by major companies such as Netflix, Amazon, and Google. By modeling user behavior and preferences, we can build machine learning models that suggest the highest priority item in the list first. For example, if you are planning to cook but only have a few ingredients, we can recommend the best recipes for you based on your previous culinary experiences (if we have that data), top-rated recipes containing the available ingredients, and sort the list from highest score to lowest score. The use cases for recommendation engines continue to grow, and flexible knowledge graphs combined with LLM-based embeddings offer a unique, scalable approach to tackle the most challenging and most valuable data problems.

Finally, we dove into the topic of fraud detection in the book. We showcased how the knowledge graph helps untangle complex fraud schemes and even helps us pinpoint the most influential bad actor within each community. The graph-based approach to solving fraud is the only viable solution in today's world of complex connections. It is only possible to uncover multiple connections between seemingly unrelated actors and clients by analyzing any and all connection identifiers, such as phone, email, bank account, IP address, and more, to highlight rich communities of fraudsters. Through the power of graph data science, we can now pass leads to investigators with fewer false positives and larger risk mitigation amounts, making the jobs for both data scientists and investigators much more pleasant.

Index

Made in the USA
Las Vegas, NV
11 April 2024

88559183R00105